Secrets of the Heart

Secrets of the Heart

Richard W. Dortch

New Leaf Press

First printing: January 1996

ISBN: 0-89221-299-3
Library of Congress Catalog: 95-69895

Unless otherwise noted, all Scripture quotations are
from the New King James Version of the Bible.

Note: Some names and places have been changed to
protect the identity and privacy of those involved.

This book has been manufactured using the exclusive
Flexibook® binding process.

Dedication

To my beloved friend, confidant,
elder brother in the faith,
and good Samaritan,

DR. ARTHUR H. PARSONS,

who walked with me
through the storm.
His words of truth became
a light in my pathway.
I understand Jesus better
having walked with him.

Acknowledgments

Every week I spend many hours hearing the heart-breaking accounts of people's troubled lives. I have learned never to be a passive listener. I have also discovered that when you give yourself to others, they always help you fulfill your dreams.

Many friends have helped me in this project.

Neil Eskelin has been a counselor and guide in each of my six books. I am constantly seeking answers and receiving help from this dear colleague and am a debtor to him for his assistance in bringing *truth* to reality.

Dan Johnson, my dear friend, has always given me help in each of the projects that I have undertaken.

Dr. Arthur Parsons, to whom I have dedicated this book, is my closest advisor and guide in all that I do. He is the chairman of Life Challenge, the crisis agency I serve that brings hope to so many tangled lives. He is the person that I am submitted to in my personal life and ministry.

My family — Mildred, Deanna, Mark, and Rich, are a part of everything I do. Each of them gives me strength and has helped in this labor of love.

Bob Brown, Bill Keller, Betty Chilcott, and Rev. Melvin Brewer, are people who contribute much to my personal life. Reverend and Mrs. Gordon Matheny are always there when I need them. My bishop, my friend, the Reverend Thomas Trask, has lived a life of truth before me. I draw so much from his leadership and guidance. Herman and Sharon Bailey have loved me and often given me the inspiration to "go on."

My attorneys are two of my most trusted friends. Mr. Mark Calloway, of Charlotte, North Carolina, has been appointed by the president of the United States as the U.S. attorney for the Western District of North Carolina. He now serves the nation in this honorable position. We continually pray for him. Mr. George Tragos of Clearwater, Florida, is a brilliant attorney, trial lawyer par excellence. I lean on him for his godly wisdom.

My publisher, Tim Dudley, is a friend who has believed in me, shared my vision, and helped carry the burden for my passion to write. Only eternity will reveal the lives that have been touched and changed because of Tim's willingness to publish the books that are so close to my heart. Jacqueline Cromartie is simply the best at bringing my books to the attention of the nation.

I realize that all we are and say is a composite of everything we have heard and learned. We take no credit for anything, but lay it totally at the Master's feet.

Contents

Introduction

I remember the night my good friend Neil Eskelin asked me the simple question, "What is it you want to say in your book?" I was writing my first book, *Integrity* — which came to be a best seller. My response to my colleague was totally transparent, "I want to write about integrity; how I lost it, and my journey back."

In the days spent on that project I came to grips with my past, and at every opportunity I asked to be forgiven by anyone who would listen. In deep humility I sought answers and made some discoveries about things I believed I knew — but did not.

After much reflection I have come to the conclusion that the most significant factor in our lives is truth. Why is it so vital? Because God is truth and every good thing in life flows from Him.

I have no messianic feelings about presenting this book. I am simply pursuing the single most important thing in life — truth.

There are some things you know you *must* do. The writing of this manuscript is one of those things. I not only followed my heart but it became a passion. As I began to write it was like an artesian well springing up within me. I knew what Jesus meant when He said, "Out of the abundance of the heart the mouth speaks" (Matt. 12:34).

As I explored the topic, I could hear Neil asking the question again, "What is it you want to say in this book?"

The answer to that question is based on these facts:

- The essence of all truth is God.
- When we violate truth we violate God, because He is truth.
- Truth is the only way to God — our path to wholeness and the one foundation of life that will stand.
- Truth is everything in our relationship to God and to others, and is central to our quest for self-discovery.
- There can be no compromises, choices, or substitutes for truth.
- Christ declared, "I am the way, the truth, and the life" (John 14:6).

Closely tied to this subject is the issue of secrecy. What we will be discussing does not concern the secrets we have confessed long ago to God or those we have acknowledged to others fulfilling the Scripture, "Confess your faults one to another" (James 5:16). Rather, we will address the deceptive nature of the secrets we hold because of shame.

I remember the day I listened to the story of a friend. There was a pounding, gripping sense within me that said, "He is not telling the truth."

I cared deeply about the man, but it was obvious to everyone but himself that deception had set in. When I met with him, he stated, "Yes, I met her at a motel several times — in different places around the country. But we did not have sex."

"That's very hard to believe," I responded. I drove

away from that meeting trying my best to assimilate what I had seen and heard. Because it was a private, confidential meeting, there was no one to talk to. No one with whom I could share my thoughts. Finally, in desperation, the words came thundering out of my mouth, "Whatever happened to the truth?"

Millions of people are haunted by questions of deception. "Why wasn't I totally honest?" "Why did I say such a thing?" "Why did I change the story?" "What will happen if the truth gets out?"

The reason I have such deep feelings concerning this topic is because there was a point in my life when I compromised the truth because I wanted to hide something, and I paid a horrible price. If, as a result of writing this treatise, I can help you avoid such a pit-fall, my time, my prayers, and my work will have been well spent.

I cannot begin to describe the total liberation and peace that comes when we step into the light. Many people accept God's grace and unconditional forgiveness, but stop at that point. They fail to move on to a total cleansing, a new life, and a deep relationship with God.

It is my prayer that as a result of reading this book you will make a commitment with me that truth, and how we deal with secrets, will be the central, driving force of your life.

For He knoweth the secrets of the heart.
— King David

1

The Letter

"Oh what a tangled web we weave, when first we practice to deceive!"

— Lord Byron

The minute the plane landed I walked to a pay phone and dialed the number of a friend I had known for many years. "This is Richard. I'm at the airport. Can you meet me here at the coffee shop? I really need to see you immediately."

"What's it about?" he asked, sensing the urgency in my voice.

"Please, just come out to the airport," I replied.

It wasn't like me to fly several hundred miles across the country for an unscheduled meeting. But that's what I felt I had to do. That same morning I purchased a round trip ticket from the city where I lived. This was a matter that couldn't be discussed by phone.

Just two weeks earlier this colleague and friend had been a guest in the church where I was the minister. Wherever I have pastored I've been big on celebrations and he was one of many we brought back for a week-long special occasion. It was an exciting time of renewal and fellowship.

Ten days later, my secretary walked into my office and laid a sealed envelope on my desk and walked out. At the time I was concentrating on another project and didn't turn my attention to it.

Later that morning I glanced at the envelope and noticed that it had been stamped "Return to sender." I recognized that it was my own stationery but someone had drawn a line through the printed return address. The letter was addressed to an individual whose name was not familiar — and I did not recognize the handwriting.

Wondering who could have used my stationery, I opened the envelope and pulled out a 10-page letter and began to read. As I reached the fourth or fifth page my heart sank. I knew that I was reading a letter written by one of the guests of our celebration to a woman friend, and that there was a sexual alliance between them. The vivid contents left no doubt of their relationship. It was also obvious that they had mutually agreed upon a post office box where they could exchange correspondence. Evidently, the woman had not picked up her mail in 10 days and it was returned to me — since the sender had not totally blackened out the church address.

I stopped reading, placed the letter back in the envelope wondering, "What should I do?"

At the time I was not a denominational official. I

was the resident pastor of a local church. I thought, *Well, the Bible tells us to confront a brother in his sin.*

That's when I decided to make the flight for a face-to-face encounter.

A Moment of Terror

"What on earth is going on?" the concerned former associate asked as we walked into the airport coffee shop.

"I'm scheduled to fly back in about two hours but there's something we must talk about," I replied as we were shown to a table.

Just after the waitress placed two glasses of water before us and went to get our coffee, I reached into my pocket and pulled out the letter. I placed it in front of him and said, "Do you recognize this?"

He stared at the envelope and I witnessed a look of terror wash over his face. His whole body tightened. Almost immediately, he grasped his stomach and said, "I'm going to vomit." He rose, and walked, stooped-shouldered, to the rest room.

It was 20 minutes before the shaken man returned. His face was ashen white — the picture of a man shrouded in shock. His secret had been exposed. The lie he was living had suddenly been brought to light.

Slowly he began to gain his composure and he asked, "What do you intend to do with the letter?"

I responded, "That is the wrong question. What do *you* intend to do with the letter?"

He sat quietly for a few moments and pondered. Then he looked at me and said, "Richard, with the way that God is blessing me, and the way this church has grown — it has almost doubled — I don't think there is anything that should be done."

I was stunned. I couldn't believe his response. It was obvious that he wanted me to keep the matter quiet. I was also convinced that he did not plan to deal with his sin. After pausing for a moment, I looked the man in the eye and said, "I wouldn't trust you with my wife or my daughter and will not turn you loose on others."

I felt an obligation to take the matter to another level. I continued, "You and I have a mutual friend" — and I mentioned the name of the person. "When I return home I am going to meet with him and share this information. I'm not going to handle this by myself." Then I added, "If you are not gone from this church within 60 days and out of the ministry for at least three years, the matter will be taken to denominational leaders."

The next day our mutual friend called, urging him to do what I had suggested.

As the 60-day deadline approached, the fallen friend phoned, saying, "I need 30 more days."

We granted him the extension, not knowing there was no willingness on his part to face the consequences of his deeds.

It was only when denominational officials confronted him and removed him from spiritual leadership that he began to deal with the deep-seated problems of his life. The man had lived with his deceit for so long that it had become part of his nature. He was filled with such pride that he believed his sin was immune from punishment. He had forgotten that there is still a God who writes upon the wall, "Mene, mene, tekel, upharsin. . . . You have been weighed in the balances, and found wanting" (Dan. 5:25, 27).

The Stunning Statistics

I wish I could tell you that in my lifetime of ministry that was the only case that has troubled me. Far from it. As a pastor, denominational official, and now as president of the national crisis agency Life Challenge, I have been privy to over 1,500 cases of failure involving people at every level of society — business executives, factory workers, government leaders, attorneys, ranchers, ministers, and lay people.

Woven into the fabric of each heart-rending story are the common threads of lies, deceit, and secrecy. That fact became clear when I was recently asked, "Richard, how many people voluntarily came to you before their transgressions were exposed?"

I thought for a moment and said, "Only about 10 percent."

Then came the second question. "How many people lied when they were caught?"

"Over 90 percent," I sadly responded.

People don't change when they see the light. They change when they feel the heat.

Sociologists James Patterson and Peter Kim, in their insightful book, *The Day America Told the Truth*, say, "Lying has become an integral part of the American culture, a trait of the American character. We lie and don't even think about it. We lie for no reason."[1]

I was amazed when I read the results of Patterson and Kim's national study — where nearly 3,000 people nationwide responded with total anonymity. They learned that:

> • 97 percent of the people surveyed
> admitted they had lied — and 91 per-

cent acknowledged lying regularly.

• Nearly one-third of all married persons (31 percent) had cheated on their spouse.

• 64 percent said, "I will lie when it suits me, as long as it doesn't cause any real damage."

• We lie most to those we love best. Eighty-six percent of lies are told to parents, and 75 percent to friends.

I was especially disturbed at the finding that "Only 1 in 10 of us believe in all of the Ten Commandments. Forty percent of us believe in five or fewer Commandments."[2] This, in a nation where 47 percent profess to be born-again Christians.

Perhaps the Psalmist was speaking to us when he wrote: "You love evil more than good, And lying rather than speaking righteousness" (Ps. 52:3).

Fakes and Phonies

How pervasive is the problem? Dr. Joyce Brothers observes that "Lying is so much a part of our lives that the average American tells some 200 lies a day. This includes 'white' lies, false excuses, lying by omission, and so on."[3]

It should not surprise us that a significant number of people feel like fakes, phonies, or hypocrites. Studies show that nearly one out of four thinks it is all right to use deceit when applying for automobile insurance and more than half of all college students indicated they had cheated on papers or exams.

According to M. Hirsh Goldberg, author of *The Book of Lies,* a human resource consulting company hired to investigate the truth about the background of job applications, found "outright lies on more than 30 percent of resumes today."[4]

The problem permeates every level of society — from the military to the media. As a result there is a growing distrust for the institutions that have been the bedrock of our democracy.

What do we tell our kids when major networks plead guilty to "faking" film footage in their so-called investigative reports, when public schools inflate their enrollment to obtain more government grants, and when the highest political officials resign in disgrace?

I read with great interest the words of Norman Isaacs, former president of the American Society of Newspaper Editors. In his candid book, *Untended Gates: The Mismanaged Press,* he admits that "There are too many who crave (the scoop) to the point that if they cannot come up with one legitimately, they are perfectly willing to invent one."[5]

Isaacs told the story of Janet Cooke, an aggressive young reporter for the *Washington Post,* whose account of an eight-year-old heroin addict on the streets of the nation's capitol riveted the attention of thousands of readers. The boy's name was "Jimmy" and her eyewitness account of seeing him injected with the deadly drug caused a stir among civic leaders. The heart-wrenching story resulted in the *Post* being awarded the coveted Pulitzer Prize.

The publicity of the prize called even more attention to the story and it was soon discovered that the entire account was a hoax. The prestigious *Post* was humiliated. It had to return the Pulitzer and try to explain how something like this could have happened.

The consequent investigation of the case revealed that Ms. Cooke not only misled the public, but had lied on her job application. She did not graduate from the college she claimed and there was no Master's program at the school she listed for her advanced degree.

It's no wonder that we have grown to distrust those who quote anonymous sources, place ratings ahead of truth, and have few guardians to enforce ethical standards.

We are quick to blame the press, the politician, or the business professional when headlines scream of fraud or deceit, yet millions of average people make a mockery of truth every day. They say things they don't mean, socialize with people they don't really like, and fail to stand up for what they truly believe. As British writer Samuel Johnson wrote in the seventeenth century, "Almost every man wastes part of his life in attempts to display qualities which he does not possess and to gain applause which he cannot keep."

What's the Problem?

Deceit takes many forms. It happens through action, inaction, gestures — even through silence. And many rationalize their deception by thinking, "If nobody is harmed, what's the problem?" To them, lying is as natural as breathing.

For example, every day highway patrolmen hear adults make up excuses of why they were speeding. "My accelerator was stuck." "My kids were driving me crazy, so I was in a hurry to get home." When one fellow saw the flashing blue light he drove even faster until he reached a service station, jumped out of the car and ran into the rest room. When he came out he exclaimed, "Sorry about that, officer. I didn't think I was going to make it."

"That's okay," the patrolman said. "I had time to write out this $72 ticket."

Deceit starts early. Any school teacher can give you a list of fibs kids come up with of why their homework wasn't completed. "The dog ate it." "My mother threw it away by mistake." "My little sister scribbled on it."

I recall the story of three boys who were seniors in high school. On a beautiful spring day they decided to play hooky from their morning classes. After lunch, the boys came to school and said, "Sorry we're late. We had a flat tire."

The teacher smiled and said, "Well, young men, you missed a little quiz we had this morning. So take out a piece of paper and sit apart from one another." Then she asked them to write the answer to this question: "Which tire was flat?"

It was a lesson they would never forget!

Perhaps somewhere there's a perfect person without a blemish on their record — they've never exaggerated their background in a job interview, never uttered a "white lie," or even nibbled a grape in a grocery store. But I doubt it. What about you?

Have you always told the truth about your age, your education, or your income? Is there a private part of you that no one knows but you? Would you truly stand up for your principles, regardless of the consequences? Do you honestly mean it when you say, "How nice to see you"? Do you give false excuses for not attending a social function? Have you ever taken credit for something you really didn't do? Are the numbers on your expense account accurate? Have you ever taken things at work for your personal use? Do you really tell "the whole story" to your spouse, your kids, or your employer? Have you ever been asked to do something at work you felt was unethical? How did you respond?

Painful Soul-Searching

Please don't think I am writing this book from a lofty perch of virtue and perfection. Far from it. If you have read my books *Integrity: How I Lost It and My Journey Back* and *Fatal Conceit,* you know that because of the wrong decisions I made in handling a confidence, I lost my health, my reputation, my ministry, and was sentenced to a federal prison. I lost almost all of my life's possessions.

It has taken me a long time to come to grips with a deception that was once in my life. Today I fully realize and admit my mistakes. I also believe that what I have learned can help you avoid falling into a trap from which there seems no escape. You must be willing, however, to look at yourself in the mirror.

What I am about to share with you is the result of the most difficult, painful soul-searching of my life. In many ways, you may find it uncomfortable, too, since we are dealing with issues that are at the core of our relationship to God and man.

On the following pages we'll discuss:

- Warning signs of deception
- Avoiding the penalty of secrets
- Keys to self-examination
- Building trust and confidence
- Escaping denial
- Keys to confession

- Finding principles worth keeping
- Ten secrets for truthful living
- Finding freedom from guilt
- Life-changing declarations of truth

You may never be compelled to fly to a distant city to confront someone who has committed a transgression. But you need to be prepared. It's important to know how to respond if a close, personal friend tells you she has just committed adultery — or if someone you love tells you he is stealing from his company — or if someone you care for confesses to living a double life.

I am convinced this is the day Jeremiah spoke of when he prophesied, "Everyone will deceive his neighbor, and will not speak the truth; they have taught their tongue to speak lies" (Jer. 9:5). The apostle Paul also declared "For the time will come when . . . they will turn their ears away from the truth, and be turned aside to fables" (2 Tim. 4:3-4).

In a world defiled by deceit and shamed by secrecy, it is my desire that this book will cause you to commit your life to the most powerful principle God has provided — the principle of truth.

2

Matters of the Heart

"I shall tell you a great secret, my friend. Do not wait for the last judgment, it takes place every day."
— Albert Camus

"Mildred, I want to go over to the church early this evening," I told my wife on a Sunday afternoon in Collinsville, Illinois.

"Why?" she wanted to know.

"I just feel I need to spend some time praying before the service," I replied.

We were visiting the town where I had spent my childhood years. Earlier, on that same trip, I made the pilgrimage to the old farmhouse where I was raised. The white wood-framed house is still standing at the pinnacle of a steep hill. When I was growing up we had no electricity or running water. I still remember what it was like to lower the tin bucket on a pulley to the bottom of our 80-foot well. Nothing compares to a drink of that cold, fresh water.

I remember that every time threatening weather approached, my father, Harry, took the family into the basement to protect us from the howling winds. Oh, how I longed for those days when I could again be shielded from the storms!

Now, after the devastating events that had rewritten the story of my life, I felt honored and humbled to be invited to once again speak in my home church.

It was a time when I was still searching for answers to what had gone so horribly wrong in my life. I thought, *If somehow I can get alone with God, I'll be able to experience once more what I remembered as a child.*

It was in that church, at the age of six, that I felt the unmistakable call on my life to ministry.

When we arrived at the sanctuary, Mildred was busy upstairs while I made my way down to the basement and opened the door to an empty Sunday school room.

Instead of simply kneeling, I decided to lie down before the Lord and I began to cry out. "Jesus," I wept, "bring me back to those childhood days, when my heart was so pure before You. How did I leave this church, knowing that You had called me to preach, and yet I stumbled and compromised my life? Lord, where did I go wrong?"

I desperately wanted God's purifying process to touch and cleanse me again. And, in an unusual way, He did.

The Rapture Factor

Those who know me best will tell you that I am not a person who sees visions and hears voices from heaven. But that evening, something unexpected happened.

As I prayed, I began to hear the distinct sounds of some very familiar voices. In my mind's eye I could actually see them — three past deacons of that church. There were Mr. Shaffer, Mr. Hamm, and my own father.

Memories flooded me as I heard Deacon Hamm say, "Brethren, let's not buy as much coal this winter because Jesus is about to come. And we don't need to spend money on all that coal when there are missionaries who are waiting for our help."

Then I saw my dad coming home after a service, saying, "Children, I gave all I had to missions tonight." I recalled the time as if it were yesterday. My father awoke about three o'clock the next morning to make some pies from the jars of fruit he had preserved in the summer. As the sun came up, the five Dortch kids were loaded up with baskets full of pies to sell for a nickel each. We survived. We saw God's provision.

Next I saw the pastor standing before the congregation on a Sunday night. At the end of his message he proclaimed, "We probably won't have a service here Wednesday, because I believe Jesus will come before then."

God allowed me to return to that place and be touched by those memories to bring me to this conclusion: **There is a vital correlation between believing in the imminent return of the Lord and our hidden life.**

That evening the message I delivered to the congregation was also for me. The Lord made me aware that when we fully realize the consequences of sin our behavior will drastically change.

Somehow, the soon return of the Lord has been pushed far from our consciousness. The Rapture of the Church and the Day of Judgment is no longer a central teaching. We have ignored the warning: "Therefore you also be ready, for the Son of Man is coming at an hour when you do not expect Him" (Matt. 24:44).

As I was growing up, we were taught that motion pictures were an evil form of entertainment and that we should not attend. We heard it from the pulpit and it was reinforced in our home. At the age of 15, however, my curiosity got the best of me. I remember sneaking off to St. Louis to see a movie. The city was just across the Mississippi River from where we lived.

When I reached the corner of Seventh and Locust, I nervously looked around to be sure no one would see me buying my ticket to the Ambassador Theater. I can even remember the movie. It was *Ali Baba and the Forty Thieves,* starring a popular actor of that day, Terhan Bey.

About 15 minutes after the film started I began to have grave misgivings about my decision. I thought, *What if my parents knew I was here? And what if the Lord came this very moment?* Filled with fear and anxiety, I literally ran out of that theater and made my way home.

Without question, there is a definite correlation between our hidden life, self discipline, and the coming of the Lord. How does our belief in the soon return of Christ affect our behavior? Scripture tells us that "Everyone who has this hope in Him purifies himself, just as He is pure" (1 John 3:3).

I am dismayed at the current lack of emphasis on this doctrine. During the past four years, ministering in churches of all sizes, only on one occasion have I heard a hymn or special song about the second coming of Christ. I shudder to think what will happen if the trend continues. Will we soon conclude that there is no consequence for deceit and no penalty for sin?

While we may no longer dictate what social activities are sinful, we tolerate sloppy living in our churches, families, and our own lives, making sure no one feels "uptight."

When you truly believe that Jesus may come today, two important things happen. First, you'll confess your sins to God. Second, you'll make things right with your fellow man.

The apostle Paul admonished us to keep our hearts "blameless in holiness before our God and Father at the coming of our Lord Jesus Christ with all His saints" (1 Thess. 3:13).

Deceived in the Garden

The seeds that have produced our harvest of deceit were planted long ago. In fact, the sin that caused the fall of man in the Garden of Eden was the result of three lies.

Lie number one: In direct contradiction of God's directive not to eat of the tree of the knowledge of good and evil, Satan, in the form of a serpent, told Eve, "You will not surely die" (Gen. 3:4).

Lie number two: Eve repeated Satan's falsehood and caused Adam to also eat of the forbidden fruit. "So when the woman saw that the tree was good for food, and that it was pleasant to the eyes, and a tree desirable to make one wise, she took of its fruit and ate. She also gave to her husband with her, and he ate" (Gen 3:6).

Lie number three: Later, Adam lied to God about his actions in violating God's commandment. Instead of accepting personal responsibility, he blamed his wife. He said, "The woman whom You gave to be with me, she gave me of the tree, and I ate" (Gen. 3:12).

When Christ walked the earth, He gave this description of Satan: "He was a murderer from the beginning, and does not stand in the truth, because there is no truth in him. When he speaks a lie, he speaks from his resources, for he is a liar and the father of it" (John 8:44).

Throughout recorded history there is a trail of lies and deceit. Surprisingly, Scripture is filled with vivid examples.

- Abraham lied when he entered Egypt and said Sarah was his sister (Gen. 12:13).
- Jacob impersonated his brother Esau to obtain his father's blessing (Gen. 27:6-23).
- Delilah deceived Samson to find the source of his strength (Judg. 16:4-20).
- David escaped from the king of Gath by pretending to be insane (1 Sam. 21:13).
- Herod was dishonest when he asked that the Christ child be found

"that I may come and worship Him also" (Matt. 2:8). In truth he wanted him killed (Matt. 2:16).

• The Pharisees lied to Jesus when they said, "Teacher, we know that You are true, and teach the way of God in truth" (Matt. 22:16). He called them "hypocrites."

• The chief priests and scribes "sought how they might take Him by trickery and put Him to death" (Mark 14:1).

• When Jesus was arrested in Jerusalem, Simon Peter denied knowing the Lord (Matt. 26:72).

• Sarah deceived Pharaoh by pretending to be Abraham's sister (Gen. 12:11-20).

What was God's solution to a world filled with lying, secrecy, and deceit? To redeem us from our sinful condition, He sent His Son, "Who committed no sin, nor was guile found in His mouth" (1 Pet. 2:22).

Seven Consequences of Deceit

Those who come to the conclusion that "A little lie won't hurt you," haven't looked closely at the laws of God. One of the Ten Commandments given by the Almighty is that "You shall not bear false witness against your neighbor" (Exod. 20:16). Later, He told the children of Israel, "You shall not steal, nor deal falsely, nor lie to one another" (Lev. 19:11).

Those aren't suggestions. They're direct orders, and when we live in disobedience there is a price to pay. Here are seven consequences we can expect.

1. Deceit harms our relationship with God.

When I was placed in the position of being trusted with a secret that could destroy an entire ministry, it had a devastating impact on my life. When I knew I had "crossed the line" and became a participant in hiding the truth, I felt that my relationship with God was in jeopardy.

Suddenly, the focus of my life shifted. I was constantly looking over my shoulder wondering what would happen next. Spiritually, I began to suffer. My prayer life, my time with God's Word, and — because of guilt — my communion with the Lord was affected.

I needed to heed what God spoke through Jeremiah: "Why then is this people of Jerusalem slidden back by a perpetual backsliding? They hold fast to deceit, they refuse to return" (Jer. 8:5). And the Lord said, "Your habitation is in the midst of deceit; through deceit they refuse to know Me" (Jer. 9:6).

2. Deceit affects our decision-making ability.

When I became trapped by secrets, it seemed that my entire thought process was changed. Was every action and every decision clouded by the hidden facts I knew? Was my arrogance and pride — trying to give the impression that "everything is under control" — keeping me from properly advising my friend during his hour of greatest need?

Inside, I was hurting. I began to doubt my ability to lead, my ability to minister, and began to wonder about my own future. Saint Augustine said, "When regard for truth has been broken down or even slightly weakened, all things will remain doubtful."

I continued to make decisions, but they were made with apprehension and uncertainty.

3. Deceit impacts our physical health.

It is impossible to calculate the physical and emotional damage caused by secrecy and deception. In addition to the hopeless feeling of being trapped and not knowing where to turn, you feel as though every ounce of energy is totally drained. You are literally "zapped."

As the tension and trauma continued to build, my health began to fail. I was frightened by my symptoms and required constant medical care. I was taking 19 pills every day.

That's what we can expect when we are not operating in truth. Deception erodes our health, emotions, and spiritual life.

Today, after escaping from my web of deception and applying the principles I am sharing with you, I have experienced a physical turn-around.

I am not taking any medication at all — none. I doubt if I take three pain pills in a year. Total freedom from deceit produces amazing results.

4. Deceit keeps us from accepting personal responsibility.

Those who have become enmeshed in dishonesty search for excuses. They blame everyone and everything — from their enemies to their environment. Talk to any defense attorney and you'll hear a long list of excuses for their client's behavior. "They were temporarily insane." "They were only protecting their rights." "They are a victim of the system."

I can vividly recall a week of television programs we ran at PTL with the theme "Enough is Enough." It was a direct attack on the *Charlotte Observer* to counter the negative stories they were publishing about the ministry. Our point-by-point refutation, however, was misguided. We should have admitted our mistakes, and spent our time and energy on improving the entire operation.

It took a long, difficult time for me to come to the conclusion that the problems I faced were not with the media, they were with me, and my deceitful attitudes and behaviors.

5. Deceit harms our family and friends.

Our actions are not isolated. They affect not only our personal life, but can deeply wound those we love the most.

Perhaps I could have withstood the unrelenting headlines of my conduct and the courtroom testimony that followed. But my heart was broken when I realized the pain it all had brought to my family.

My daughter, Deanna, suffered incredible hurt when the attacks on my reputation occurred. Every rumor and accusation was like a dagger through her heart.

I could have easily understood if my son, Rich Dortch, with an M.B.A. from Duke University, had asked to change his name. Everywhere he turned he was asked, "Are you any relation to Richard Dortch?" But he stood with me through my darkest hour.

Only heaven knows what my wife, Mildred, has endured. Tears alone can never measure her heartache and grief. I can never repay her devotion, but I will spend the rest of my life trying.

6. Deceit leads to a pattern of dishonesty.

It is almost impossible to tell only one lie. To cover deception you have to invent new scenarios, give false impressions, and present additional falsehoods to bolster your position.

For many people, the deception is so pervasive that their memory is on constant alert. The moment they see a friend they think, *What did I tell them?* How much easier it would be if we lived by the rule: "If you always tell the truth, you never have to remember what you said."

We have often heard the comment, "He's a born liar." But that's not the case. We *learn* to tell untruths and it becomes a moral choice. Truth, over time, becomes what we choose it to be.

By constant repetition, and before we realize what is happening, deceit can become a permanent part of our life. Sissela Bok, professor of ethics at Harvard Medical School, says, "After the first lies . . . others can come more easily. Psychological barriers wear down; lies seem more necessary, less reprehensible; the ability to make moral distinctions can coarsen."[1]

7. Deceit always brings punishment.

As surely as the sun rises in the east, God will bring punishment to those who disobey His commands.

I have often been asked, "Richard, why did you plead guilty in the PTL case?"

My answer is simple. "I pleaded guilty because I was guilty."

No, I wasn't guilty of all the things for which I was originally charged. But I agreed to take full responsibility for the mistakes I had made. I was given a sentence for my actions.

Many are deluded into believing that their deceit will remain hidden and their secrets will never be revealed. They are wrong. The sentence begins at the moment of the act — with the torment of your heart and the guilt of your conscience.

It is also true that today, or even tomorrow, is not the final day of reckoning. There is a moment coming when our entire life will be revealed. "For we shall all stand before the judgment seat of Christ" (Rom. 14:10).

There was a time in my life when I was virtually destroyed by deceit. As I told a friend, "I had become a master at shutting down my own conscience."

God not only got my attention, He revealed where I had gone wrong and showed me the pathway back. Again, I am drinking the clear, refreshing water of truth that springs from His deep, deep well. And He is providing shelter from the storm.

3

The Secrets about Secrets

"Three may keep a secret if two of them are dead."
— Benjamin Franklin

"Richard, are there any deep, hidden things in your life that may have caused you hurt and pain?" Dr. Alfred Fireman asked. Mildred and I were seated in the Florida office of this professional psychiatrist and counselor. We were trying to sort through the crisis that had invaded our life.

At that very moment a grand jury was investigating my activities and I was living in fear of being stalked by the media. Television crews from ABC, NBC, and CNN were frequently parked near our house, wanting my comments on breaking news stories surrounding the PTL events.

Dr. Fireman kept probing. "Is there something you've never told anyone? Something you may have carried with you all of your life?"

"Yes, there is," I confessed.

"Do you want to talk about it?" the psychiatrist asked.

"Sure. You may think this is trivial, but it certainly isn't to me. Dr. Fireman, I have never understood why, for all of my life, people have called me by a name that I was never given. And it has bothered me more than anyone will ever know."

As a boy I was called "Dick" and I always despised the name, but I never reached the point where I could talk about it. It was my secret. I couldn't understand why everyone in my family was called by their given name, but it seemed I was the exception. I thought, *If my name is Richard, and I always sign my name that way, why don't people just call me "Richard"?*

I recalled the time I was invited to speak to a large church conference. It was a big moment for me — a young minister about to speak to thousands of my peers from across the nation. Then, when the person who was presiding walked to the podium to introduce me, I started to cringe. He began talking about "Dick Dortch."

The counselor encouraged me to bring my secret to the surface and I can now smile about a topic that troubled me for so long. I must admit, however, that I still despise the nickname. Last Christmas my wife — for the first time — put "To Richard" on the card attached to my gift. I really did appreciate it. After all, that's my name.

Perhaps there is something hidden in your life that has caused great distress. It may be something you have witnessed, an act for which you have great regret, or knowledge of an event you would like to forget. In this chapter we will discuss the truths we attempt to conceal. They're called *secrets!*

The Three Levels of Secrets

Have you ever seen an envelope stamped with the words "PRIVATE!" or "CONFIDENTIAL"? If you are like me, you are itching to know what the letter contains. In many cases, the words are stamped simply to cause us to read the information. If it were truly private, the matter might have been handled in person; not written on paper.

Secrets can be either good or bad, moral or immoral, truthful or deceitful. It's how we handle them, however, that makes the difference. Let me identify three distinct levels of secrecy.

Level One: Discretions.

I have secrets in my life that I believe are appropriate. I call them discretions.

• What a man and wife does privately, unless it is breaking the law, should be no one's business but theirs.

• What is discussed among family members should remain private.

• Business matters between employer and employee should be confidential.

Discretions are permissible secrets.

Level Two: Confidences.

It is vital that we have someone to whom we can confide — to share our inmost secrets and with whom we unburden our heart. We may be seeking sound advice or simply need a listening ear.

Physicians, attorneys, counselors, and ministers fulfill that role professionally. These trained professionals practice by a code of conduct, so we feel comfortable sharing our secrets. For example, there are individuals who would not discuss the details of their investment portfolio with their children, but freely share every detail with a banker or estate planner. And medical doctors often know more about a patient's body than the person would tell their family.

There is another arena where confidences may occur — but seldom do. It is on a personal level. We should all have a friend with whom we can be totally transparent. Is there such a person in your life? Is there someone with whom you can be brutally honest and admit your most personal weakness?

In a later chapter we will deal with the guidelines of Scripture for "confessing our sins one to another." The topic is vital because most of us are not obeying the Word on this issue. Why isn't it happening? We hesitate to confess our faults because of a basic lack of trust. The same problem exists for both leadership and laity. We simply don't have someone in whom we can totally confide — someone whom we trust to not betray our confidence.

True friendship and trust don't develop overnight. Begin now to identify the person who has the potential to fill this important role in your life. And ask yourself if you are willing to fulfill this role in the lives of others.

Level Three: Undisclosed thoughts and acts.

Now we come to the "danger zone" of our secrets — those things known only by you and the Almighty.

Except for an omniscient God, there is no one who knows the real you. No one knows what you read, what you listen to, or your activities behind closed doors. No one knows your secret thought life.

It's amazing how the behavior of many people drastically alters when they are in a distant city — where no one knows them or cares about their actions. In such situations people continually run risks they would never chance if they were known.

The question we need to ask is: "What would happen if this knowledge was revealed?" Sadly, the answer is often: "I would be humiliated and disgraced."

Discretions and confidences protect us, but true secrets are the result of shame. We need to examine our actions so there will be no *need* for harboring things that could lead to a lifetime of regret.

Helpers Need Help, Too

Being involved in crisis counseling I can tell you that the person who shares a secret is often less burdened than the one with whom the confidence is shared. On so many occasions I have felt the weight of the problem shift from their shoulders to mine.

A married man from Indiana — an accountant — tearfully confessed that he had been carrying on a homosexual liaison with a man in a neighboring city for more than three years. As he left my office after our initial visit he shook my hand and said, "Pastor Dortch, you'll never know how much better I feel by sharing this."

He may have been relieved, but because of my deep concern for him I was troubled. I knew the trauma his wife and family would face before his profound problems would be resolved.

One of the dilemmas faced by people of good will is that we want to be a true confidant to people who are living through times of distress. Before God, we desire to be a faithful steward of what they share. We strive to do whatever it takes to protect and shield those we care about from harm or reproach. But in doing that, we often ensnare ourselves.

After I had given a presentation to a group of attorneys in New York, a lawyer asked to talk with me privately. He said, "While you were speaking it dawned on me that while I constantly listen to confidential matters, I have never, ever shared my secret problems with another person. I have become my own confessor."

The same problem exists for psychologists, medical doctors, and those in the clergy. Since they are trusted "secret keepers" they rationalize that they are the best people to deal with their own personal problems. The decision is not because of a professional commitment, but they have transferred this whole concept of confidences to hide their own private sins.

A counselor needs a counselor. A minister needs a minister. A physician needs a physician. I am reminded of the words of a song that says "We all need somebody to lean on."

Six Secrets About Secrets

What do we need to know about hidden matters of the heart? What are the danger signs and warnings? How do we effectively deal with secrets?

Here are six things to remember.

Secret Number One: Keep confidences confidential.

A confidence should remain just that — a confidence.

I remember attending a party while I was in junior high school and we played a game called "rumor." There was only one rule for the game. The first person was to whisper something to the person on his or her right and they were to repeat the information to the next person. Well, as you can imagine, after the secret had been passed to 20 kids around the room the final statement was far different from the first.

That's what happens when a confidence is broken. The wild rumors — usually untrue — that follow can often cause permanent damage to someone's reputation. Never forget that false information thrives in an atmosphere of gossip and idle talk.

If someone asks, "Please don't share this with anyone else," make a vow that you will keep that commitment, and keep your vow. Few people realize the strength of character and reputation that surrounds those who have learned to keep private matters private. They are not only trusted, but admired.

Secret Number Two: Beware of hidden motives.

Because of our basic human need for fellowship it is easy to become caught up in an organization or social group that is actually a "movement" with a secret agenda. We should constantly ask, "What are the motives of the leadership of this group? What are they seeking? Is it personal power, financial gain, social change, political leverage, religious indoctrination?"

Literally millions of well-intentioned people have been pulled into dangerous cults because they had no idea of the real intentions of the leaders. Suddenly they were caught up in everything from sexual perversion to terrorist activities. One woman, after being "deprogrammed," said, "I can't believe I was so fooled.

They seemed like such caring people."

Undisclosed motives can be found everywhere — in the teaching profession, in politics, in labor organizations, and in the media.

On several occasions I've had the privilege to talk with the noted actor Efrem Zimbalist Jr. He once told me, "Those who believe that Hollywood simply wants to expose people to things they haven't seen before, don't know how it operates. They have a secret agenda. They want to change the world."

Don't allow yourself to become a pawn in another person's game. Ask as many questions as it takes to find the truth before aligning yourself with a project, an organization, a church, or a social cause.

Secret Number Three: God knows the real you.

At every level of society there are people who have a "fake it 'til you make it" mentality. In their counterfeit world of pretense they try to disguise the flaws in their life. But they can't hide from God. He knows exactly who they are, what they believe, and the intent of their heart. Yes, God knows the real you!

> • He looks beyond your exterior.
> "For the Lord does not see as man sees;
> for man looks at the outward appearance, but the Lord looks at the heart" (1 Sam. 16:7).

> • He looks beyond your words.
> "Now what more can David say to You?
> For You, Lord God, know Your servant"
> (2 Sam. 7:20).

> • He knows your inmost secrets.
> "You have set our iniquities before You;

Our secret sins in the light of Your countenance" (Ps. 90:8).

• He knows your thoughts and intents. "For the word of God is living and powerful, and sharper than any two-edged sword, piercing even to the division of soul and spirit, and of joints and marrow, and is a discerner of the thoughts and intents of the heart" (Heb. 4:12).

• He even knows our "inclinations." Speaking of the children of Israel, God said, "For I know the inclination of their behavior today, even before I have brought them to the land of which I swore to give them" (Deut. 31:21).

• You cannot hide from Him. "And there is no creature hidden from His sight, but all things are naked and open to the eyes of Him to whom we must give account" (Heb. 4:13).

As the Psalmist wrote, "If we had forgotten the name of our God, Or stretched out our hands to a foreign god, Would not God search this out? For He knows the secrets of the heart" (Ps. 44:20-21).

Secret Number Four: Constantly self-examine your heart.

In every pharmacy you can purchase a kit to check your blood pressure, record your cholesterol level, or measure your temperature. But there's nothing available to examine the secrets of your heart. It is something for which you have been given total responsibility.

We may attempt to mask our feelings with clever conversation but the person deep inside somehow rises to the surface. It's true. Jesus declared, "For out of the abundance of the heart the mouth speaks" (Matt. 12:34).

Why are we commanded to look deep within? "Keep your heart with all diligence, for out of it spring the issues of life" (Prov. 4:23). The Lord said, "From within, out of the heart of men, proceed evil thoughts, adulteries . . . covetousness, wickedness, deceit" (Mark 7:22).

Jeremiah warned about those whose "tongue is an arrow shot out; it speaks deceit; one speaks peaceably to his neighbor with his mouth, but in his heart he lies in wait" (Jer. 9:8).

When our heart is right, everything else about us becomes right. I love the advice given by the apostle Peter. He said, "Do not let your beauty be that outward adorning of arranging the hair, of wearing gold, or of putting on fine apparel; but let it be the hidden person of the heart, with the incorruptible ornament of a gentle and quiet spirit, which is very precious in the sight of God" (1 Pet. 3:3-4).

Secret Number Five: Never stop searching for truth.

After years of counseling and in dealing with my own shortcomings, I am convinced that *when we know what our secrets are, we know what our problems are.* That's why we should never abandon our quest for reality and truth.

The Psalmist asked these important questions,

"Lord, who may abide in Your tabernacle? Who may dwell in Your holy hill?" (Ps. 15:1). And he gave the answer: "He who walks uprightly; And works righteousness; And speaks the truth in his heart" (Ps. 15:2).

Many people attempt to bury their mistakes and block their memory from reality. But it doesn't work. If the problem is not dealt with openly and in truth before God, the issue will surface in a variety of ways.

What does the Word declare? "Only fear the Lord, and serve Him in truth with all your heart; for consider what great things He has done for you" (1 Sam. 12:24).

Secret Number Six: Live in total honesty

I once heard about a woman who mailed an anonymous money order for $300 to the Internal Revenue Service. Attached was this note: "I cheated on my income tax last year and have not been able to sleep since. This check covers half of what I owe. If I continue to have trouble sleeping, I will send you the rest."

A little bit of integrity is not enough. Only 100 percent will do. Otherwise it's like trying to bake a cake with only half of the ingredients. It simply won't work.

By being honest with ourselves we can be honest with the world. Do you remember reading Shakespeare's *Hamlet*? There is a point where a father says to his son, "This above all; to thine own self be true, and it must follow, as the night the day, thou cannot then be false to any man."

From the beginning of time, the Lord has provided exactly what we need to cope with the issues we face. "The secret things belong to the Lord our

God, but those things which are revealed belong to us and to our children forever, that we may do all the words of this law" (Deut. 29:29).

That's His plan for addressing the matters of our heart.

4

Shackled by Shame

*"No ear can hear nor tongue can
tell the tortures of the inward hell!"*
— Lord Byron

It was Good Friday, April 17, 1986. But it was
not good for me.

It had been several weeks since Jim Bakker resigned from PTL, but the glare of the media spotlight
was beaming with more intensity every day. We had
warnings for several days that the *Charlotte Observer*
was about to publish another blockbuster story — but
we just didn't know when.

On that Friday night I told one of my assistants,
"I want you to go down to the loading dock of the
Observer and get an early edition of tomorrow
morning's paper." I knew that about 10 o'clock they

would be loading the trucks that carried the state edition of the paper to news distributors across the Carolinas. I said "Bring me the copy immediately."

That evening Mildred and I attended the Heritage USA Passion Play — a spectacular presentation that was opening for another season. As the moving drama ended I saw the assistant standing at the top row of the amphitheater. He had a newspaper in his hand.

I rushed up the steps and nervously asked, "Well, what does the article say?"

"I don't think you're going to like it," he replied as we huddled in a corner where no one could see me anxiously scanning the story.

I made an instant decision. "Here's what I need you to do," I told the young man. "Tomorrow morning, find some people to help you and buy up every copy of the *Charlotte Observer* within a two-mile radius of Heritage USA. Go to the newsstands, the grocery stores, the fast food restaurants — I don't want anybody to see this story."

I knew this front page feature would be devastating. For the first time, the world would know the intimate details of the inner workings and the compensation of the top executives at PTL — including me.

On Sunday morning I would be standing before 2,500 people at the Heritage Village Church and preaching to a live national television audience. How could I face them? What would they think? I couldn't bear the thought of having something so private become the conversation of millions of people.

My secret was about to be revealed and I was mortified.

Since that day of revelation I have spent a great deal of time examining my heart. I had to admit to myself and to the Lord that while I was a denominational leader, and then as an executive at PTL, I never wanted my compensation revealed. I was strident on the issue. I insisted that every protection possible be built into those procedures to guarantee secrecy on that matter. At one point I was even successful in having the board pass a resolution that salaries would not be divulged.

Today, when I look back on my actions, there was only one reason I didn't want those things revealed. I was ashamed.

Oh, I could make the case that if I were on a comparable corporate level I would be deserving of such a large salary and perks. But I was not working for IBM or Exxon. I was working for Christ, who taught, "Whoever desires to come after Me, let him deny himself, and take up his cross, and follow Me" (Mark 8:34).

I was not the president of NBC, I was an executive at PTL. And as an official of my denomination, I was not running General Motors, I was working in the kingdom of God.

It is permissible to keep personal confidences, but there should be nothing about our work that we should be ashamed to disclose.

The Real Test

Often, I have been asked, "Richard, how can we know the difference between 'acceptable' secrets and those that cause injury or harm?"

The ultimate test as to whether a secret is harmful is your answer to this question: *Does my secret bring me shame?*

Why did I want the newspapers to "disappear?" They were about to expose information I had successfully been able to protect as confidential. Facts I had tried to keep hidden were suddenly being revealed and I was embarrassed.

Please don't conclude that all secrets are harmful. They're not. But we need a measuring device to warn us of danger. Just because we fail to disclose something doesn't mean our behavior is improper. For example, you don't tell your child about a birthday gift that is hidden in your closet. Or you don't need to reveal the fact that your boss has confidentially told you he's resigning at the end of the fiscal year.

Was Winston Churchill ashamed that he devised a plan for espionage agents to infiltrate Nazi Germany during World War II? Did his actions cause guilt and remorse? No. This was war and he knew that spying was necessary.

But what about the college student who spends an hour reading her roommate's private diary without permission? Should she feel ashamed? Absolutely. The coed will know in her heart that what she has done is wrong.

A High Price to Pay

Recently, a man who was vacationing in Florida called our Life Challenge office and said, "How soon can I make an appointment to talk with Richard Dortch? I need to see him immediately."

Three days later I was able to meet with him — a distinguished gentleman in his late fifties. The moment I looked at him I sensed something was wrong. "The reason I needed to talk with you is because of my involvement in a business venture that is causing me a great deal of distress," he began.

When I learned the facts, I could understand his anguish. The man was a road planner for a state highway department. A friend who was an investor in commercial real estate came to him one day and asked, "How would you like to be a partner in a land development project?"

"I don't have that kind of money," he laughed.

"No. You don't need any money at all," the friend explained.

For revealing the location of a proposed interstate interchange, the investor would give him 20 percent of the profits on the land he would secretly purchase at today's prices and later resell.

"I made a horrible decision," the man confessed. "I entered into the off-the-record agreement and I have been deeply troubled by it ever since." He told me about his sleepless nights and the profound torment his decision had produced.

During our conversation he agreed that to accept even one penny for his inside information would only compound his problem. However, he was still struggling with the knowledge that many unsuspecting land owners had already sold their property to the man and would be cheated out of the skyrocketing value of their property when the road's location was announced.

Even *before* you make a decision, ask yourself, "Is there a possibility that guilt or remorse will accompany the truth I am hiding?" If the answer is "Yes," run from the activity as far and as fast as possible. Perhaps Will Rogers said it best: "I would rather be the man who bought the Brooklyn bridge than the man who sold it."

The shame caused by our secrets has a far greater impact than we realize. Noted psychologists Frank Minirth and Paul Meier say, "Shame is at the root of all addictions. It may be forgotten, hidden, or disguised, but the shame is there, it is real, and it drives behavior."[1]

Minirth and Meier have found that those involved in compulsive behavior are attempting to cover their deep-rooted remorse — and that shame and addiction are always found together, even though one may come to the surface first. In my crisis counseling I have observed that this link is always present.

Guilt caused by deceit takes a variety of forms. Many parents have lied about their wedding date to keep a child from knowing he or she was born out of wedlock. A spouse will often "cover" for a mate who is an alcoholic by attributing an unsteady walk or slurred speech to prescription drugs for some other problem.

Where Can I Hide?

To better understand the roots of remorse and the seeds of shame we need to look again at what happened in the Garden of Eden. Earlier we talked about the three lies told by Satan, Eve, and Adam. But what were the results of that deceit? What behavior was produced?

Immediately, after attempting to deceive the Creator, "The eyes of both of them were opened, and they knew that they were naked; and they sewed fig leaves together and made themselves coverings" (Gen. 3:7). The first man and woman were so ashamed that they "hid themselves from the presence of the Lord God among the trees of the garden" (Gen. 3:8).

Adam confessed that after hearing God's voice in the garden, "I was afraid" (Gen. 3:10). Not only was he ashamed, his heart was filled with fear.

A similar fate befell Jonah when he tried to hide from God by fleeing to the city of Tarshish. When a violent storm threatened to break up the ship, they cast lots to determine who was responsible for the tempest. All eyes turned to Jonah. He admitted his guilt and said, "Pick me up and throw me into the sea; then the sea will become calm for you. For I know that this great tempest is because of me" (Jon. 1:12).

Today, the shame caused by our secrets continues to plague us.

When my world came tumbling down and I began to walk through my personal hell, I had an extremely difficult time facing the world. At the peak of the major crisis of my life I was being ridiculed in the press, by the public, and even in some pulpits. My ever-present thought was, *Where can I run to and hide?* I felt like the Psalmist, who wrote: "Have mercy on me, O Lord, for I am weak; O Lord, heal me, for my bones are troubled. My soul also is greatly troubled; But You, O Lord; how long?" (Ps. 6:2-3).

"I am weary with my groaning; All night I make my bed swim; I drench my couch with my tears" (Ps. 6:6).

When I was dismissed from my duties in Charlotte we hurriedly moved to Clearwater, Florida. But there was no escape. Not only did the national stories continue, but the local media crowned me with the kind of celebrity you wouldn't wish on anyone.

One day Mildred tried to get me to walk with her

through the Countryside Mall. I drove her to the parking lot and said, "I think I'll just stay here in the car." Whether it was true or not, I felt that every eye was looking at me.

Finally, I summoned enough courage to walk into a public restaurant for the first time. But the minute we were seated, my eyes became moist and I confessed, "Mildred, I'm not ready for this." We hurriedly left the cafe.

After being in the ministry for so many years I thought that perhaps someone would stop by and say, "Richard and Mildred, we just want you to know that we love you." In those first dreadful days, it didn't happen. When I was an asset to the church I was showered with kindness. But now I was a liability and I felt isolated and alone.

Out of Excuses

For nearly five months I couldn't bring myself to attend a Sunday church service. There were, however, two couples who opened their hearts to us — Robert D'Andrea and his wife, Molly, and Herman and Sharon Bailey, hosts of "Action Sixties," a popular TV program.

On several occasions the Baileys had invited us to attend the large evangelical church where they were members. I made excuses each time. Finally, early one Sunday morning, Herman called and said, "Richard, you and Mildred are going to church with us today. We'll be there to pick you up at ten o'clock."

I tried one of my usual excuses but this time it didn't work. "I won't take 'No' for an answer," Herman insisted. "We want you to be our guests today."

I was very uncomfortable as we slipped into a

pew at the Pinellas Park Wesleyan Church. Then something unusual happened. Just before the message, the minister asked a young woman named Mindy to come to the front. The girl, in her twenties, literally ran to the platform as the entire congregation stood to their feet in applause. Then, the pastor presented her with *two* bouquets of red roses.

As we were seated I wondered, *What has she done to deserve all of this attention?*

The pastor explained, "Mindy, you have been gone for two and a half years, and many of these people don't know who you are." Then he told how this lovely girl from their church had been involved in an accident where alcohol was present and had just been released from the Florida Prison for Women.

"Mindy, how many of these people have written to you or visited you since you went to prison?" the minister asked.

I'll never forget her answer. She smiled and said, "Pastor, I quit counting after a thousand."

At that moment I knew we had found a church home — a warm, loving group of people who would be a shelter in our time of storm. They didn't point fingers or pass judgment. They simply reached out to embrace us when we needed it most.

Herman Bailey was used by God to literally rescue me from my shame. It was a great landmark on my road to recovery and I will be forever grateful.

Finding an Escape

How can you find freedom from guilt and remorse? Here are seven steps to your release from harmful secrets.

1. Identify your errors.

Be realistic about faults and failures. Many people have "imagined" or false guilt. It is not based on fact, but on feeling — and can be extremely dangerous, leading to a wide variety of destructive behavior.

Remember, Satan will accuse you of far more than you are truly guilty of as he attempts to makes us feel unworthy of God's favor and forgiveness.

The process of recovery begins when you zero in on *real* failure. Solve those problems first.

2. Admit your mistakes.

Don't shift the blame. Take full responsibility for your actions. Listen to what the Psalmist wrote. "Wash me thoroughly from my iniquity, and cleanse me from my sin. For I acknowledge my transgressions: and my sin is ever before me" (Ps. 51:2-3).

3. Renounce harmful secrets.

The apostle Paul, extremely concerned with false teachers who had come to the city of Corinth, wrote: "We have renounced the hidden things of shame, not walking in craftiness nor handling the word of God deceitfully, but by manifestation of the truth commending ourselves to every man's conscience in the sight of God" (2 Cor. 4:2).

4. Confess your transgressions to the Lord.

Every act that produces guilt and shame is contrary to the requirements of God's Word. Receiving pardon from yourself may be important, but nothing compares to having your iniquities removed by God himself.

David was guilty of deceit, adultery, and even murder. But God forgave him because He was genuinely repentant. He wrote, "I sought the Lord, and He heard me, And delivered me from all my fears" (Ps. 34:4). He saw the same results in others: "They looked to Him and were radiant, And their faces were not ashamed" (Ps. 34:5).

5. Confess your mistakes to a trusted friend.

Immediately, find a pastor, a counselor, or a friend to whom you can confide. Scripture tells us to "Confess your faults one to another, and pray one for another, that you may be healed" (James 5:16).

Sharing the hidden areas of your life is much more than a symbolic act. Cleansing comes when darkness is brought into light.

6. Ask forgiveness of those you have harmed.

The process of restoration requires that you not only face God and yourself, but that you make things right with those you have caused harm. You may have to travel 10 miles or 10,000. It doesn't matter. Find the injured party and say, "I know my actions have harmed you. I am truly sorry. Will you please forgive me?"

Jesus declared, "Forgive, and you will be forgiven" (Luke 6:37).

7. Start walking on a new path.

Your freedom may require that you break free from old habits and routines. And you may need to surround yourself with new friends who are affirming and supportive.

Now is the time to say "Farewell" to those things which have caused you regret and remorse. If God can bury your secrets forever in the deepest sea, so can you. Remember the Lord makes it possible to become a new creation. "Old things are passed away, behold all things are new" (2 Cor. 5:17).

After emerging from the shadows of my darkest gloom, I have made a commitment to God and to myself that I will never again become associated with anything that has the slightest tinge of shame.

What about you? Is there something happening in your life that is causing regret or remorse? You may say, "Oh, it's nothing." Harmful secrets, however, are like poison. One hidden thought or deed may not seem dangerous, but when they begin to multiply the results are deadly.

Start now to remove your shackles of shame.

5

Practicing Humility

"God resists the proud, and gives grace to the humble" (1 Pet. 5:5).

Leighton Ford, a man who reached out to me in my pain, likes to tell the story of a new factory owner who went to lunch at a small neighborhood restaurant which featured a "blue plate special." It allowed for no substitutions.

When the executive asked for a second pat of butter the waitress refused. Irritated, he called for the manager, but she also refused him.

"Do you know who I am?" he asked indignantly. "I am the new owner of the factory across the street."

The woman smiled and retorted, "Do you know who I am, sweetie? I am the person who decides whether you get a second pat of butter!"[1]

In a world crowded with people who flaunt their self-importance, we need a few more such bubble-busters.

For many people, money, power, and prominence are like intoxicating drugs. Before long, the rules that govern society are for someone else, not them. They demand — and usually get — tickets to events that are already sold out. They illegally park in spaces marked "Handicapped" without giving it a second thought. Even when they bend or break the regulations of their own profession there is often nothing more than a slap on the wrist. We've all heard the stories of sports super-stars who hire and fire coaches, decide how many minutes they will play, and set their own salaries.

If you were to ask some people to draw a picture of the world, they would place themselves at the center. As Winston Churchill said about a haughty, conceited colleague, "There, but for the grace of God, goes God."

A person may wear dark sunglasses, reside behind a security gate, and have an unlisted telephone number, but God knows more than our name, our address, and how to reach us. "He knows the secrets of the heart" (Ps. 44:21).

To say that power and fame are seductive is an understatement. I should know. It happened to me.

After years of ministry in the United States and Europe I was suddenly thrust into the national spotlight of daily television. "This sure is different than pastoring in Garden City, Kansas," I told a friend one day as we milled through the crowds on "Main Street" at Heritage USA. At its peak, more than six million visitors a year were coming to the popular tourist attraction.

When the flashbulbs are popping and you are signing autographs for Aunt Mabel and Uncle Bill, your view of reality is somehow distorted. As I later told a writer for *Christianity Today*, "A television camera can change a preacher quicker than anything else. It turns a good man into a potentate. It's so easy to get swept away by popularity. Everybody loves you, cars are waiting for you, and you go to the head of the line. That is the devastation of the camera. It has made us less than what God has wanted us to become."[2]

A Revealing Connection

You may ask, "Richard, what does vanity and conceit have to do with truth? Can't those who have a high opinion of themselves still be people of honesty and integrity?"

The issue here is not high versus low — but higher than others. We forget the equality of God's eyes. When your view of yourself becomes inflated it tends to twist and warp everything else, too. Reality is no longer relevant and the line between fact and fiction becomes hazy and blurred.

Here's the conclusion I have reached: *Deceit and secrecy thrive in an atmosphere of pride and arrogance.*

How closely are these factors linked? There is a revealing list of things God hates found in the Book of Proverbs — things that are "an abomination to Him" (Prov. 6:16-18).

Specifically, the Lord despises:

1. A proud look
2. A lying tongue
3. Hands that shed innocent blood
4. A heart that devises wicked plans
5. Feet that are quick to rush to evil
6. A false witness who speaks lies
7. A man who stirs up discord among brothers

What is number one on God's "most hated" list? Pride. Not only does He detest it, He will punish it. "The Lord will destroy the house of the proud" (Prov. 15:25). God isn't interested in wounding our pride — He wants to crucify it — daily.

Recently, I counseled a woman in her early sixties whose world was falling apart. She was separated from her husband after more than 30 years of marriage and was not on speaking terms with her children.

It seemed that every question was answered with, "It's all his fault," or "You don't know what my daughters have put me through." Because of her pride, she had convinced herself that her woes were the result of flaws in her family. It was some time later when she finally brought herself to admit, "I suppose I've made some mistakes, too."

Keep Looking Up!

Self-deception is not only found in the private dining room of a corporation, the locker room of a sports arena, or on a Hollywood movie set. It has infiltrated the Church.

I have met scores of Evangelicals and Charismatics who have developed a sense of spiritual superiority. Some are so convinced they have a corner on truth that they refuse to fellowship with those who haven't "seen the light." Others who claim to possess a supernatural gift are often condescending toward those they feel have not reached their own godly plane.

Spiritual snobbery is fraught with danger. If *we* become the truth, where does that leave God?

Several years ago I spoke at a convention that chose three simple words as its theme: "Keep Looking Up!" Such advice could save us from a great deal of trouble. As C. S. Lewis wrote, "A proud man is always looking down on things and people; and, of course, as long as you're looking down, you can't see something that's above you."[3]

Whether you are outside or inside the walls of the church, "Pride goes before destruction, and a haughty spirit before a fall" (Prov. 16:18).

Once, while having lunch with a group of businessmen, our conversation drifted to the subject of pride. One fellow commented, "I think it's interesting that when God created man, He constructed our body to make it virtually impossible to pat ourselves on the back."

Another man smiled and added, "It may look impossible but I know a lot of people who manage to do it!"

How wonderful it would be if more people would heed the Scripture that declares: "Let another man praise you, and not your own mouth; a stranger, and not your own lips" (Prov. 27:2).

Have you ever attended a social gathering and been "cornered" by someone who is intent on telling you every glorious detail of his latest exploits? I have. When it happens I am reminded of the old adage: "Pride is the only disease known to man that makes everyone sick but the one who has it."

Dave Thomas, founder of Wendy's International, states, "There are some people you just can't stand. I'm suspicious of people who brag a lot. The quiet ones who listen well are often the best managers. The ones who interrupt you mid-sentence and who seem self-important can cause you real grief."[4]

Some individuals aren't content with gloating about yesterday, or even today. They chatter endlessly about grandiose plans for the future and list accomplishments they have yet to achieve. Obviously, they haven't read the warning: "Boast not of tomorrow, for you don't know what a day may bring forth" (Prov. 27:1).

It's time to let our actions do the talking. Being raised on a farm, I learned long ago that the hen that lays the largest eggs is not always the one doing the most cackling.

Who Can We Follow?

What is the answer to the problem of pride? How can we avoid the traps caused by a disregard for truth and honesty? The answer is wrapped up in one word — *humility!*

Fortunately, in God's Word we can find some excellent role models.

We need the humility of Abraham.

The man who was called the "Father of Israel" knew his rightful place before God. When the Lord was about to destroy the city of Sodom, Abraham looked up to heaven and said, "Indeed now, I who am but dust and ashes have taken it upon myself to speak to the Lord" (Gen. 18:27).

We need the humility of Jacob.

On his journey to be reconciled with Esau, Jacob said to the Lord, "I am not worthy of the least of all the mercies and of all the truth which You have shown Your servant" (Gen. 32:10).

We need the humility of Moses.

When God revealed His great mission to a man who had been herding cattle in the desert, Moses was humbled. He asked the Lord, "Who am I that I should go to Pharaoh, and that I should bring the children of Israel out of Egypt?" (Exod. 3:11). And when God asked him to speak to the people, Moses responded, "O my Lord, I am not eloquent, neither before nor since You have spoken to Your servant; but I am slow of speech and slow of tongue" (Exod. 4:10).

We need the humility of Solomon.

As Solomon was about to ascend to the throne, he admitted his shortcomings by declaring, "Now, O Lord my God, You have made Your servant king instead of my father David, but I am a little child; I do not know how to go out or come in" (1 Kings 3:7). Asking for wisdom and knowledge, he asked God, "Who can judge this great people of Yours?" (2 Chron. 1:10).

We hail Solomon as a great builder, but he questioned, "Who am I . . . that I should build Him a temple?" (2 Chron. 2:6).

We need the humility of John the Baptist.

John became a "a voice in the wilderness" to announce the coming Messiah but he didn't boast of his accomplishments. He declared that the One who was coming "is mightier than I, whose sandal strap I am not worthy to stoop down and loose" (Mark 1:7).

Do you remember the scene at the Jordan River when Jesus asked John to baptize Him? John tried to deter Him, saying, "I have need to be baptized by You, and are You coming to me?" (Matt. 3:14).

We need the humility of the apostle Paul.

The man who wrote nearly two-thirds of the New Testament and boldly preached the Gospel to the world, served the Lord "with all humility, with many tears and trials" (Acts 20:19). He confessed, "For I know that in me (that is, in my flesh) nothing good dwells" (Rom. 7:18). He came to the Corinthians "in weakness, in fear, and in much trembling" (1 Cor. 2:3).

We need the humility of Jesus.

Christ stood before the large crowd that gathered on the Mount of Olives and declared: "Blessed are the meek, for they will inherit the earth" (Matt 5:5). Later He said, "Take My yoke upon you and learn from Me, for I am gentle and lowly in heart, and you will find rest for your souls" (Matt. 11:29).

Here's how Paul described the nature of Christ: "And being found in appearance as a man, He humbled himself and became obedient to the point of death, even the death of the cross" (Phil. 2:8).

Seven Benefits

A life insurance salesman once told me, "When I'm selling a policy, people don't seem interested in the history of the company, its outstanding leadership, or even its financial stability. They only want to know one thing, 'What are the benefits?' "

God makes commitments, too. When it comes to

humility, there are seven great rewards.

Benefit Number One: You'll receive honor.

How would you like to be granted any wish you desire? That's what God promised Solomon when he was about to become king. The newly named leader had only one request. It was for a wise and understanding heart.

God responded that because he had "not asked long life for yourself, nor have asked riches for yourself, nor have asked the life of your enemies, but have asked for yourself understanding to discern justice," his wish would be granted (1 Kings 3:11).

Then, the Lord did something even greater. He said, "And I have also given you what you have not asked: both riches and honor, so that there shall not be anyone like you among the kings all your days" (1 Kings 3:13).

Benefit Number Two: You'll have abundance.

It was true in the life of King Solomon, and it is still a promise for today: "By humility and the fear of the Lord are riches and honor and life" (Prov. 22:4).

Benefit Number Three: You'll receive wisdom.

There's a great difference between being smart and being wise. It takes much more than a university degree to be qualified to make good decisions. Wisdom is a byproduct of humility. "When pride comes, then comes shame; but with the humble is wisdom" (Proverbs 11:2). But there is also this warning: "Let not the wise man glory in his wisdom" (Jer. 9:23).

How did James ask us to conduct our lives? We are to act "in the meekness of wisdom" (James 3:13).

Benefit Number Four: You'll receive grace.

A meek spirit unlocks the doors to God's storehouse — including His unmerited favor. Scripture says that the Lord "scorns the scornful, but gives grace to the humble" (Prov. 3:34).

Benefit Number Five: You'll receive blessings.

Are you seeking God's best for your life? Here's the prescription that never fails: "If My people who are called by My name will humble themselves, and pray and seek My face, and turn from their wicked ways, then I will hear from heaven, and will forgive their sin and heal their land" (2 Chron. 7:14).

Benefit Number Six: You'll be lifted up.

People are often surprised when they ask God to make their travel plans. The route to the top of the mountain often requires that we start at the bottom of the valley. As James wrote, "Humble yourselves in the sight of the Lord, and He will lift you up" (James 4:10).

What Jesus told His disciples is still true. "If anyone desires to be first, he shall be last of all and servant of all" (Mark 9:35).

Benefit Number Seven: You'll experience God's presence.

You may wonder, "How can I have God's touch on my life? How can I receive His anointing?" It begins when you turn your back on pride, arrogance, and conceit. God told Isaiah, "I dwell in the high and holy place, With him who has a contrite and humble spirit" (Isa. 57:15).

These seven benefits are only the beginning of what a life of humility will bring.

A reporter once asked Billy Graham: "You've

preached to more people in your lifetime than any man in history. How do you explain your success?"

Graham thought for a moment and responded, "Sir, the only explanation I know is God."

"But why," asked the reporter, "did God choose you?"

Billy smiled and said, "When I get to heaven, that's the first question I am going to ask Him."

That's humility.

6

Beware of Little Foxes

"I have never killed a man, but I have read many obituaries with a lot of pleasure."
— Clarence Darrow

I'll never forget the first time I saw the Grand Canyon. It was far bigger than I imagined. *What could have caused such a gigantic rift in the earth?* I wondered.

I learned that the immense canyon wasn't created overnight. The flowing water of the Colorado River etched the gorge by removing just one grain of sand at a time. I was even more amazed to discover that the vast Mojave Desert in California was created by the same sand the river carried downstream.

Perhaps you have visited an underground cave

like Meramec Caverns to view the amazing displays of nature called stalactites and stalagmites. These icicle-shaped masses are formed over centuries by the calcium deposits of tiny beads of water — one drop at a time.

Most of us go through life searching for answers to the big issues we face. At the same time, however, we may be undermined by small forces that pose a far greater danger. The small problems surface everywhere.

> • The launch of a manned space flight has to be scrubbed because of a small rubber seal that won't properly close.
> • A famous auto racer loses the Indianapolis 500 because a tiny wire in his ignition system fails.
> • A few almost invisible termites sneak into the woodwork and destroy the foundation of a luxury home.
> • One small mutant cell multiplies until an entire body is plagued with deadly cancer.
> • One small rivet on the wing of a giant aircraft breaks, causes additional fractures, and the jet crashes.

Long ago, Solomon, one of the wisest men who ever lived, spoke these insightful words: "Catch for us the foxes, the little foxes, that spoil the vines: for our vines have tender grapes" (Song of Sol. 2:15).

As we will discover, he wasn't talking about small

animals that were ruining someone's crops. The "foxes" of which Solomon spoke were the secret sins that cunningly ravage our lives and harm our relationship with God.

It's easy to only focus on major issues. An anti-abortion rally can draw 200,000 crusading protesters to the nation's capitol. Mother's Against Drunk Driving (MADD) can enlist more than a million members nationwide. A crusade against juvenile crime can gain national television exposure. But where are the protesters against the subtle snares of hate, envy, lust, or lying that are pulling people apart — literally from the inside out?

We need to understand the difference between sins of the flesh and sins of the spirit. Adultery, murder, and drunkenness are overt acts that can attract a great deal of attention. Yet what about those things we can't see, such as a man who has a burning hatred for a business rival, or a woman who is obsessed with thoughts of sexual perversion? Just because we can't "see" the sin doesn't make it less of a moral offense. The same spiritual rules apply. As Paul so forcefully wrote, "Those who practice such things will not inherit the kingdom of God" (Gal. 5:21).

Three Little Foxes

There are enemies that will sneak into your garden — almost unnoticed — and rob you of your harvest. You need to be on constant alert for these three invaders.

The First Little Fox: Harmful thoughts.

Just as a tiny acorn can produce a mighty oak, a simple idea that enters your mind can become an all-encompassing giant that takes total command and dominates your life. I've seen the havoc caused by simple thoughts that grow and multiply until they are out of control. It especially happens in the areas of egotism, jealousy, and dwelling on impure thoughts.

The danger of an inflated self-image can't be over-emphasized. It's been said that, "many a bee has drowned in his own honey."

Equally as damaging is jealousy. I doubt there's a person alive that has not experienced a twinge of envy. A small boy thinks, "I sure wish I had a little red wagon like that." A teenage girl wonders, "Why does Mary get all the dates?" An assistant manager thinks, "Why was he promoted and not me?"

What happens when envy turns to hate and rage? I was sickened when I read the story of a mother who became involved in a murder plot because someone else was chosen to be a high school cheerleader rather than her own daughter.

The advice of the apostle Paul was direct and to the point: "Let us not become conceited, provoking one another, envying one another" (Gal. 5:26).

We also need to guard our mind from impure thoughts. How is that possible? The moment an unin-vited evil thought enters your mind, immediately re-place the idea with something positive. "Whatever things are true, whatever things are noble, whatever things are just, whatever things are pure, whatever things are lovely, whatever things are of good report, if there is any virtue and if there is anything praise-worthy; meditate on these things" (Phil. 4:8).

The Second Little Fox: Harmful words.

During World War II a poster was prominently

displayed in factories producing military hardware. It read, "Loose lips sink ships!"

The average person, who speaks over 25,000 words a day, is seldom fully aware of the impact his or her words can have. Criticism, gossip, and distortion of facts have become the common denominator in far too many conversations.

Theses "sins of the lip," are the result of an unruly, undisciplined tongue. James wrote that the "tongue is a little member and boasts great things. See how great a forest a little fire kindles!" (James 3:5).

It is almost impossible to totally repair the damage caused by just one unfounded rumor. For example, a woman in Pennsylvania who taught at a day care center had a "run in" with the mother of one of the students. Later that day, the mother became so upset and angry she suggested to one of her friends, "I wouldn't be surprised if that woman was a child molester."

Before long, the phone lines in that city were buzzing that the woman *was* molesting children. Even though there was not one shred of evidence to back up the charge, the woman's reputation was ruined beyond repair. She became the object of endless suspicion and finally the family had to leave the city.

Here's a prayer we desperately need to pray. "Deliver my soul, O Lord, from lying lips and from a deceitful tongue" (Ps. 120:2) "Set a guard, O Lord, over my mouth; Keep watch over the door of my lips" (Ps. 141:3).

The Third Little Fox: Wrong actions.

Just as a thought or a careless word can injure and wound, the small acts of our behavior speak volumes. It happens when we conduct ourselves in a way that causes an onlooker to conclude that we have an unclean heart or a wrong spirit.

I remember a conversation I had with a young minister who was experiencing a great deal of conflict between himself and the official board of his church. "There's a spiritual battle going on here that is much larger than the people involved. They don't understand the principles of leadership and authority," he told me.

Then, when the chairman of the board gave me their side of the story, it was altogether different. "This fellow is giving us great concern," he explained. "He's extremely rude to his wife in public, berates his children continually, and seems filled with bitterness and anger."

The turmoil — that had started as a minor event in his childhood — had bubbled to the surface and was affecting everyone with whom he came in contact. Finally, the troubled minister was dismissed from his pulpit duties and his congregation gave him the funds to enter a professional counseling program.

The three small foxes we've discussed may seem trite and irrelevant. Yet in God's sight, sin is sin. Just as there is no such thing as a "small murder" there is no such thing as a "white lie." You either are truthful or you are not.

The Warning Signs

Everywhere we turn there are messages of caution. "Beware of falling rocks." "Please fasten your seat belt." "The Surgeon General has declared that this product is dangerous to your health."

The admonition to "beware of little foxes" should also be taken seriously. Small things are only big things in disguise. They may seem insignificant, but looks can be deceiving. Quoting the philosopher Cicero, "The beginnings of all things are small."

To determine if any small dangers are at work in your life, let's look at the warning signs. Are you guilty of any of the following?

> Repeating unfounded gossip.
> Stretching the truth to make a better impression.
> Bragging about your personal activities.
> Continually thinking of someone you secretly despise.
> Being envious of the possessions of others.
> Being obsessed with sexual fantasy.
> Justifying your own small transgressions you know are wrong.

Four Ways to Defeat the Foxes

Our problems, no matter how trivial, need to be dealt with immediately. Here are four things you can do to overcome the assaults on your life.

1. Learn the secret of bearing fruit.

Here's good news. You don't have to fight the battle alone. There is protection available for the fruitfulness of your life.

When you have a personal relationship with Christ, you'll understand that it's impossible for the little foxes to destroy the vine. Why? Because Christ said, "I am the true vine, and My Father is the vinedresser" (John 15:1).

He is the vine and we are the branches. The Lord

tells us: "Abide in Me, and I in you. As the branch cannot bear fruit of itself, unless it abides in the vine, neither can you, unless you abide in Me" (John 15:4).

The secret of bearing fruit that lasts is to draw your nourishment from the true vine. He not only feeds us, but provides total protection. We are to put on "the armor of light . . the Lord Jesus Christ, and make no provision for the flesh, to fulfill its lusts" (Rom. 13:12-14).

2. Sow to the Spirit.

Not only is Christ our vine, He sent the Holy Spirit so that the work He began in us would continue. As Paul wrote, "Walk in the Spirit, and you shall not fulfill the lust of the flesh" (Gal. 5:16).

What crops can we expect when harvest time comes? "The fruit of the Spirit is love, joy, peace, longsuffering, kindness, goodness, faithfulness, gentleness, self-control. Against such there is no law" (Gal. 5:22-23).

The law of sowing and reaping cannot be avoided. If you plant greed that's exactly what you'll get. There is, however, a crop you can cultivate that will never fail. "For he who sows to his flesh will of the flesh reap corruption, but he who sows to the Spirit will of the Spirit reap everlasting life" (Gal. 6:8).

3. Go fox hunting.

The next time your mind, your heart, or your actions are invaded, don't hesitate. Declare war.

That's what Samson did when he wanted to destroy the enemy. The Bible tells us that "Samson went and caught three hundred foxes; and he took torches, turned the foxes tail to tail, and put a torch between each pair of tails" (Judg. 15:4).

4. Take control of little things.

James explains that we only need to put a small bit into the mouth of a horse: "They may obey us, and we turn their whole body" (James 3:3). Then he said, "Look also at ships: although they are so large and are driven by fierce winds, they are turned by a very small rudder wherever the pilot desires" (James 3:4).

It doesn't take a mighty torpedo loaded with a powerful warhead to sink a battleship. The vessel will sink if there is only one small hole in its side that isn't repaired. The water begins to seep in, and if it goes unnoticed, may sink the ship

I'll never forget hearing C. M. Ward deliver a message on the dangers of dishonesty. He declared: "The laws of God act together in perfect harmony. Always let your heart, your head, and your conscience form a straight line. The moment we begin to allow our notions of policy, or even humanity, to modify or rule our notions of right and wrong, sincerity and deceit, we open a door to abuses no man can shut."

Keep the door to your mind guarded, and locked, to every invading force of your life. Remember, Jesus said, "I chose you and appointed you that you should go and bear fruit, and that your fruit should remain" (John 15:16).

With His help, you can overcome the little foxes.

7

Stepping into the Light

"For there is nothing hidden that will not be disclosed, and nothing concealed that will not be known or brought out into the open." — Luke 8:17

One of the great lessons of the dangers of lies, deceit, and secrecy is revealed in the life of Joseph. He was a dreamer who loved to wear his coat of many colors. Perhaps because of their own guilt, 10 of his brothers grew extremely jealous of Joseph and conspired to murder him. They said, "Come therefore, let us now kill him and cast him into some pit; and we shall say, 'Some wild beast has devoured him.' We shall see what will become of his dreams!" (Gen. 37:20).

There he was, in an empty cistern, left to die. At

that moment the brothers saw a caravan of Ishmaelites on their way to sell their wares in Egypt. One of the brothers said, "What profit is there if we kill our brother and conceal his blood? Come and let us sell him to the Ishmaelites, and let not our hand be upon him, for he is our brother and our flesh" (Gen. 37:26-27). So they sold Joseph into slavery for 20 shekels of silver.

To cover their deed, the shameful brothers slaughtered a goat, dipped Joseph's robe in the blood and took it to their father Jacob. The father recognized the robe and cried, "It is my son's tunic. A wild beast has devoured him. Without doubt Joseph is torn to pieces" (Gen. 37:33).

What a Surprise!

For 22 years the brothers got away with their despicable act.

Meanwhile, Joseph life in Egypt was changing greatly. Because of his interpretation of the king's dreams, Pharaoh appointed him to be governor over the entire nation.

Then, because of a great famine in Canaan, Jacob sent his sons to Egypt to buy much needed grain. Little did they know that the only person who could release the grain was their own brother. When they bowed before him, "Joseph saw his brothers and recognized them, but he acted as a stranger" and accused them of being spies (Gen 42:7).

Now Joseph had a secret, too!

Unaware of who they were speaking with, and fearing for their lives, the hearts of the brothers became riddled with remorse. They became so haunted by their conscience that they said to one another, "We are truly guilty concerning our brother, for we saw the anguish of his soul when he pleaded with us, and we would not hear; therefore this distress has come upon us" (Gen. 42:21).

Finally, after a series of events that brought them to their knees, Joseph revealed himself. His brothers became terrified in his presence.

But he comforted them, saying, "But now, do not therefore be grieved nor angry with yourselves because you sold me here; for God sent me before you to preserve life" (Gen. 45:5). Joseph knew that because of his position, he could save Canaan from the devastating famine.

The brothers threw themselves before him and offered to be his slaves. But Joseph saw the matter in an entirely different light. He said, "You meant evil against me; but God meant it for good, in order to bring it about as it is this day, to save many people" (Gen. 50:20).

Dr. R. T. Kendall, minister of the West-minster Chapel in London, commenting on this story, says, "For Joseph to say 'God meant it for good' was the easiest thing he ever did. He had forgiven them long, long before.

"What is more, Joseph was thinking beyond the sphere of this present, earthly journey. When we become enamored with heaven, there is no place for holding a grudge."[1]

The great principle of this account is that when everything was made known the cleansing came — and the needs of Joseph's family were supplied.

Out of the Darkness

It takes only a casual observer to recognize that everything God does, He does in the open. But the actions of the enemy of our soul are often done in secret. It's much more than coincidence. Satan represents darkness and God represents light. As a result, the issue of secrets is central to our affinity with the Almighty since it indicates the path we choose.

In Jerusalem, Jesus told the skeptics, "While you have the light, believe in the light, that you may become sons of light" (John 12:36).

We need to ask ourselves a serious question. "Why should there be anything in our lives that we could not willfully share with our peers — with our brothers and sisters in Christ?" After all, what is the real need for secrecy?

Sadly, I have come to realize that some secular people that we often despise can be more open and transparent than Christians. In many cases, the press we like to call "liberal do-gooders" seek the truth no matter where it may take them. And they are not ashamed of their activities. Their job is to bring things to light — and interestingly, that is the same reason Christ came into the world.

On more than one occasion I hid from the press because, at the time, I was seeking shadows rather than sunshine. There were things I didn't want people to know.

Why did Jesus love the truth so much? Because He *is* the truth. He boldly declared: "I am the way, the truth, and the life" (John 14:6). And truth is light.

When you search for truth you'll find it. Here's how Jesus illustrated the point. "The lamp of the body is the eye. Therefore, when your eye is good, your whole body also is full of light. But when your eye is bad, your body also is full of darkness" (Luke 11:34-35).

We know that "no man can serve two masters" (Matt. 6:24). The principle applies equally to God and Satan, truth and deceit, light and darkness.

A Haunting Memory

I vividly recall the time I traveled to Rochester, Minnesota, to meet with Jim Bakker at the prison where he was assigned. It was the first time I had the opportunity to talk with him about the events at PTL that had been so traumatic for both of us.

Jim and I discussed a particular day that I had driven from Heritage U.S.A. to the editorial offices of the *Charlotte Observer*. Charles Shepard, the investigative reporter who had spent years covering PTL, had many concerns and I did my best to walk through his minefield of questions.

I asked Jim, "Do you remember me coming back to your office after that meeting? The matter we discussed was whether I told Shepard how many lifetime partners we had at PTL."

Jim recalled that on several occasions in the early stages of the project we had mentioned the number of lifetime partners, but the practice was not continued. It should have been a sign that something was wrong when we started keeping secrets. I have asked myself many times, *Why didn't we want the public to know these facts?*

That has been a haunting memory.

The charges against us had nothing at all to do with the Jessica Hahn incident. The case centered on lifetime partnerships, which the prosecutors believed were oversold.

What was our problem? Our secrets. As one of my attorneys commented, "It is more than likely that

no law would have ever been violated if every week
you had gone before the cameras and told the public
how many units of lifetime partnerships existed."

I agreed. Perhaps there never would have been a
case. The supporters of the ministry would probably
have rejoiced at the growing number of partners. Why
is this so important to me now? Because it is central to
my failure, and perhaps yours. What are we hiding?

If you look at the major legal trials that have involved government and commerce from Watergate to
Wall Street, they have not been centered on the origi-
nal actions of the accused, but the cover-up and deceit
that followed.

Richard Nixon did not resign because of his
knowledge of a theft at the Democratic headquarters,
but for lying about what he knew.

Distorting the Facts

Cover-ups not only happen in Washington and
New York, they have become a way of life in both
profit and non-profit organizations across the nation. One large financial organization with offices
worldwide drastically altered the policies of its investment program that involved countless millions
of dollars. Either because of error or gross misman-
agement, the thousands of people who were relying
on the funds were never told that the organization
had failed to make necessary changes mandated by
the government. When several of the participants
were monitored, the trustees of the fund denied the
rules had ever changed.

One well-placed observer commented, "If this issue were ever allowed to be discussed in an international forum it would destroy the entire program."

Today, because directors of this vast corporation were unwilling to step into the uncomfortable light, people have been greatly penalized and thousands are in the dark as to why big changes were made in their investment program.

Of course, no one likes to hear of trouble, but when it is revealed we have an obligation to swiftly and honestly deal with it — regardless of the consequences. If the problem of the company had been dealt with in its earliest stages, it would have never grown into the dilemma it has become.

Most people understand a quick admission of our mistakes, because we have all made them. When the deception grows, however, it reaches a point of no return.

It should not be necessary for an upright organization, large or small, to keep secrets that have the potential of causing shame.

A Time for Disclosure

"Do you swear to tell the truth, the whole truth, and nothing but the truth so help you God?" That question has been asked by courtroom judges for generations.

The answer is always the same: "I do."

My experiences of the past decade have taught me many valuable lessons, but nothing comes close to the necessity of "coming clean" before God and man.

That's why I am such a promoter of the need for open, full, immediate disclosure. For example, I pray that the day will come soon when every shred of information presented to the 16-month PTL grand jury will be made public — even though some of the material may be harmful or embarrassing to me.

Disclosure has a way of bringing cleansing and release. Even those who told only part of the truth will experience a new freedom when the entire matter is revealed.

Why am I not afraid? Because I have already exposed myself to the light of the truth and have asked forgiveness of everyone who will listen. Even more, I have accepted the worst part of my life as factual and have dealt with it. Only those who continue to hide from the truth should have any apprehension.

It is astonishing to me that decades after the assassination of President John Kennedy there are still documents that have never been made public. We should not be surprised that conspiracy theories continue to abound.

After spending thousands of hours conducting church business meetings and counseling individuals I have made some interesting observations. In particular I have learned that the most important issue is the one nobody wants to talk about. The "burning issue" is usually the last one to be discussed.

In most sessions, there is more than an hour of what I call "pitter and patter." For 40 years I have counseled people who have discussed everything under the sun — the weather, the color of their kid's clothing, or where they are planning their next vacation. Finally, we get to the problem: Susie's mad because Johnny's spending the money for the wrong things.

Often, in a church business meeting, just when it's time to close the session, someone will raise their hand in the back of the room and say, "I have just one more question" — and the entire room is ignited with the confrontational issue they came expecting to discuss. One such meeting lasted until after two in the morning.

Don't hesitate. Reveal what needs to be shared. When God spoke through the prophet Jeremiah concerning Babylon, He said, "Declare among the nations, Proclaim, and set up a standard; proclaim, and do not conceal it" (Jer. 50:2).

The Coming Revelation

Sooner or later, expect the secrets of your life to be revealed.

The attorney who presided over an early settlement in a national scandal said, "No one will ever know, it's a secret." But God knew. And before long millions of people knew, too.

Jesus told the 12 disciples not to worry about those who accuse them. He announced, "Therefore do not fear them. For there is nothing covered that will not be revealed, and hidden that will not be known" (Matt. 10:26).

God has His own timetable. He may choose to reveal our secrets now, or wait until the final judgment. You can be certain, however, they *will* be revealed. "For God will bring every work into judgment, including every secret thing, whether it is good or whether it is evil" (Eccles. 12:14). As the prophet Daniel declared, "But there is a God in heaven who reveals secrets" (Dan. 2:28).

When we stand before Christ, nothing will remain hidden. On that day, "God will judge the secrets of men by Jesus Christ" (Rom. 2:16).

Paul told the Christians at Corinth that when the Lord comes, He will "bring to light the hidden things of darkness and reveal the counsels of the hearts" (1 Cor. 4:5).

The brothers of Joseph, and those who have followed their path of secrecy, have learned the painful lesson that "He who covers his sins will not prosper, but whoever confesses and forsakes them will have mercy" (Prov. 28:13).

What a wonderful feeling to escape the dark shadows of deceit and step into the rays of God's glorious light.

8

A Circle of Confidence

"Pity the man who falls and has no one to help him up!" (Eccles. 4:10;NIV).

Resigning from my post as a denominational official and becoming chief operating officer of PTL was a monumental decision for me and my family.

I was moving into an arena that was far different than anything I had experienced. Yes, it was ministry, but instead of supervising hundreds of ministers, I would be guiding the day-to-day activities of nearly 2,000 staff personnel and a non-stop building program of gigantic proportions.

The day before I assumed my duties as president of the sprawling worldwide ministry, I received an unexpected telephone call. It was from Richard Foth, who was then president of Bethany College in California. He told me that he and Dr. Richard Dobbins from Ohio, and Allen Groff from Texas, two prominent ministers and psychologists, were flying to PTL to be with me during my first days in office.

I consider these three men to be among my closest friends and I was humbled by their gesture. When they arrived, Dr. Dobbins said, "Richard, we did not come to be guests on the television program. We came because we love you. We will be here for you for whatever reason you need us."

When the four of us got together it was a like a family reunion. Many years earlier we had taken our first steps in ministry and had kept in close contact through the eventful times of our lives. I have always had great respect for each of them. Together again, we laughed and cried at our joys and sorrows. Now they had come to my side, offering their support at a time when the weight of tremendous responsibility was being placed on my shoulders.

"I'm sure there will be some rough days ahead," said Richard Foth as we sat together in a private dining room. "You know we're as close as the nearest phone."

"Is there anything specific we can pray with you about?" asked Allen Groff.

"No. Things are going fine," I replied. "But you know I am always grateful for your prayers."

Like Heavy Stones

I was not being honest with my friends. At that very moment the storm clouds were building at PTL. There were things I was learning that gave me more than a little concern. My stress was not from working long hours — I had always done that. The pressure I felt was because of the weight of secrets that were becoming like heavy stones on my heart.

Oh, I shared a few things with these men to let them know how much I truly trusted their wisdom and advice. But I couldn't bring myself to talk about the full nature of my — and PTL's — problems.

Every time I think about the arrival of my friends I say to myself, *Richard, how could you have been so foolish?* The Lord sent people to me to whom I could have told anything in total confidence without the slightest worry. But I didn't.

What kept me from doing what was right? It was my pride and arrogance. Not only did I keep my secrets from them, but I led them to believe that everything was all right. Pride has a way of distorting reality to such an extent that you eventually don't want to confide in *anyone.*

All through my life and ministry I have known that a part of my nature is to desire power, make a name for myself, to gather attention around me, and to have my own way. Sometimes I have conquered this desire; sometimes it has conquered me. I am deeply troubled by it because I know I am never more like the enemy of my soul than when I thirst for power.

If I had been candid, I would have admitted to Dobbins, Groff, and Foth: "Gentlemen, it's true that I'm president of this ministry, but I am totally over my head in what we're dealing with now and I need help." I didn't want them to see a chink in my armor or hear me acknowledge my weakness. After all, I was Richard Dortch and had the answer for everything.

I have often wondered, *Would history have changed if I had been honest and forthright about what I was harboring inside?*

Reaching Out

God doesn't intend for us to travel this road alone. That's why He created a partner for Adam and surrounded Jesus with 12 disciples. Scripture tells us to:

- Submit yourself one to another
  (Eph. 5:21).
- Admonish one another (Col. 3:16).
- Serve one another (Gal. 5:13).
- Be kind one to another (Eph. 4:32).
- Forgive one another (Eph. 4:32).
- Comfort one another (1 Thess. 4:18).
- Edify one another (1 Thess. 5:11).
- Pray one for another (James 5:16)
- Have compassion one for another
  (1 Pet. 3:8)
- Love one another (John 13:34).
- Minister one to another (1 Pet. 4:10).
- Confess your faults one to another
  (James 5:16).

How can we miss the point? It's obvious that when we see someone who is hurting we are to reach out to them. When we have a need, we should grasp the hand that is offered in love. Christ, who has all power and can do whatever He wishes, understood the importance of unity and strength. He said, "Where two are three are gathered together in my name, there am I in the midst of them" (Matt. 18:20).

A Matter of Trust and Judgment

One of the great tragedies of today's world is that

we have failed to establish the relationships necessary to make practical use of God's mandates. Even those who have a tight circle of friends don't always share what is really in their heart. People tend to believe they will be judged and rejected if they reveal their true selves, warts, struggles, etc.

During a conversation with a man in Los Angeles, he began to tell me about a crisis he was facing at his place of business. Suddenly he paused. "I don't know why I'm telling you this," he exclaimed. "I've never told another living soul."

"Do you have any close, personal friends?" I asked.

"Yes, I do. But I have never shared this with them," he admitted.

"Why not?" I queried.

"To be honest," he said, "I don't think I could trust them to keep it a secret."

If the medical, legal, and counseling professions are guided by codes of confidentiality, why can't a small group of individuals — even two or three — establish similar standards? It's something that is missing from our society.

We need to bring to the body of Christ those same kinds of commitments found in the professions. The Church, of all places, should be a haven of total trust and confidence. As Dr. Richard Dobbins says, "A safe place for everyone is when you let your humanity hang out."

Think of the anguish that could be avoided if men and women were able to confide in a close friend: "You need to know that I am struggling with greed." Or, "I need to talk with you about something. I have lust in my heart."

A moment of such candor is much more than a humbling experience. When two people are able to "talk out" a potential problem, it's like defusing an explosive device. We establish accountability the moment the discussion takes place.

I believe the reason we have ignored God's command that we "submit ourselves one to another" is because we don't see models of comparison. For example, we rarely have a living example of spiritual leadership standing before lay people saying, "I want you to know that I carry out God's Word as it relates to confessing my transgressions to another person."

Why isn't this a normal practice for clergy? As one minister sadly confided, "How can I trust another person when I can't trust myself?"

When America was being founded, young ministers received their training by being an apprentice at the feet of an older, wiser, seasoned clergyman. Every day, the older minister would spend time teaching, advising, counseling, and encouraging. Emphasis was on character, integrity, and establishing standards of ethics and excellence.

We desperately need a return to mentors in ministry and role models for lay people.

If I had made it a practice during my lifetime of having people to whom I could bare my soul, it would have saved me a great deal of suffering. There were many times I could have said, "I need your help. Will you help me? There's something going on in my life that makes me uncomfortable — something I need to share with you."

Playing With Fire

Another reason people don't form confidential

relationships with others is because they rationalize their behavior to the point that sin is no longer sin. Some individuals feel they haven't done anything that merits true confession.

There is a theory prevalent among many evangelical Christians that says, "We can come close to a transgression, but as long as we haven't actually crossed the line everything is okay." For example, there are those who believe, "I can have a sexual liaison that includes nudity as long as there is no actual penetration." They rationalize, "What I did was not really sinful because I did not have intercourse."

The Bible states that God will judge the motives of our heart. He knows our intent and will deal with us accordingly. Again and again we need to read the words of the apostle Paul, who wrote, "If we would judge ourselves, we should not be judged" (1 Cor. 11:31). In our heart of hearts we know the difference between right and wrong. We can't continually play with fire without eventually being burned by the flame.

I am doing my best to guard every thought and action of my life and to be honest about my weaknesses. I am convinced that we can avoid moral failure if there is someone to whom we can discuss our temptation. My wife and I have a commitment to each other: *no secrets!*

There's no other way to become worthy of trust than to mean exactly what you say. If someone tells you something in confidence, look at them and say, "I promise to never mention that to another soul without your permission."

The next vow you make must be to yourself. You've already made a promise to your friend, now make the same resolution to *you!* If you say you're never going to reveal the matter, make that a final decision. Remember, just one breach of a confidence sows seeds of distrust that will last a lifetime. You can never expect to have the total trust of that person again.

If the crisis you are dealing with involves only you and one other person, go directly to that individual and solve the issue there. You don't address a problem with Robert by sharing the matter with Robin. "He who covers a transgression seeks love, but he who repeats a matter separates the best of friends" (Prov. 17:9).

I would rather hear words of correction from either a friend or an enemy than to have someone say, "I love you," and then fail to point out my faults to me. As the writer of the Book of Proverbs states: "Open rebuke is better than love carefully concealed" (Prov. 27:5).

The Safety of Submission

In an age when men and women seek their own counsel and shelter their true feelings, everyone needs to be asked this question: "To whom are you accountable?" Or, "Is there an individual to whom you submit yourself?"

You may ask, "Isn't that a dangerous practice that leads to abuse?"

I know you can find examples where someone has deliberately misused their power, but what I am talking about is a healthy, open relationship where the trust and confidence is beyond reproach.

Here are four vital things that happen when we submit ourselves to someone else.

1. We protect ourselves from fatal errors.

There is a net of safety stretched beneath our lives when we are able to make decisions with some other person. A wise counselor or authority figure doesn't say, "Do it my way or else." Instead, there is almost always mutual agreement before action takes place.

2. A sense of order and discipline is established.

I remember hearing a politician from New York City declare, "I wish every home in our city could be operated with the rules of the Army, Navy, or Marines. It could make order out of chaos."

We may not have the authority of the military, but we can know what it means to live in total surrender to God and to others. When a clear line of authority is established we know where to turn for guidance.

3. We set a positive example.

The moment we establish a relationship with someone, others begin to watch our lives. The fact that you admit, "I don't have all the answers," can be the go-ahead signal that is needed for others to walk the same path.

4. We gain favor in God's sight.

The Lord expects us to follow in His footsteps. Just as the Son came "to do the will of the Father," we need to submit ourselves, too. The line of authority leads directly to the throne of the Almighty.

God has commanded us to turn to others for help.

Don't Wait!

Today, I am involved in crisis counseling. I am not usually dealing with a matter until it has reached a level of white-hot intensity. In many cases much damage has already been done and people are asking me to help put their broken lives back into place.

Don't wait for the volcano to explode before you seek assistance. At the first rumbling, run for help.

As a result of what I have seen, let me offer this counsel to young couples. Please, I plead with you to protect your lives against sensual sins. Never allow familiarity with other couples or individuals to become out of control. Be honest with your mate and discuss matters openly.

There's also something I want to address to people who have been involved in church life for many years. Don't allow your wisdom and experience to be wasted. If you are a mature leader in the church, you have an obligation to encourage and instruct. How will younger people learn unless you help them? This is a responsibility you have to God and to His people.

Why is it vital that you surround yourself with people who will listen, reflect, and offer sound advice? "Where there is no counsel the people fall: but in a multitude of counselors there is safety" (Prov. 11:14).

Don't expect miracles overnight. Honest relationships at any level are difficult to establish and maintain, but you need to say, "Look, we're going to hang in there until it is accomplished."

It took me far too long to understand how desperately I needed to establish a confidential alliance with someone. Thank God, that has happened.

I am grateful that today, the Lord has allowed an individual to come into my life with whom I can share my transgressions and failings. His name is Arthur H. Parsons and he knows the secrets of my soul.

With my Lord, my wife, and now Arthur Parsons, I know what it's like to experience the comfort, safety, and strength of a circle of confidence.

9

Escape from Denial

"Be sure your sin will find you out" (Num. 32:23).

"Bill, I am deeply concerned about these stories that have been circulating about you," I told the man who was seated in my office. I had known the gentleman for years and considered him to be a friend. Unfortunately, this was not the first time I had broached the subject with him.

"Why do these stories keep cropping up?" I wanted to know.

"I've told you before," he assured me, "there's absolutely no truth to any of it!"

The meeting on this day, however, was different. I could no longer talk in generalities. A specific accusation had been made against him and I knew I had to encounter him as a friend and brother.

For the next hour he totally denied every element of the allegation. "I don't know why people make up these stories!" he stated. According to him there was no immorality, no collusion, and no cover-up.

Toward the end of that meeting it dawned on me that I needed to detach myself from the fact that I had known this man for so long. The issue we were dealing with was much larger. I realized that my proper role was to address the problem from the correct spiritual context. I was not there representing Richard Dortch or even a denomination. I was an agent of the church of Jesus Christ to confront a man who quite possibly was involved in an immoral sexual liason.

Immediately, I leaned forward and looked directly into his eyes and said, "You need to know that my discussion with you is not on the basis of our friendship and not because of the position I hold for the moment. The questions I'm asking are not on my own behalf, but on behalf of the kingdom of God."

The man looked down and didn't say a word. I continued, "If you choose to deceive me there is no consequence. But if you are lying to the Church there will be a price to pay." I reminded him of what happened to Ananias and Sapphira when they lied to the Holy Spirit.

Fumbling for words, he offered another denial but anguish, apprehension, and distress was etched on his countenance. He walked out of my office wrapped in a cloak of gloom.

Less than two hours later my telephone rang. It was my friend, who had driven about 100 miles toward his home. "Richard," he cried, "I cannot go another mile. I'm guilty. My secret has found me out."

Those words, as painful as they must have been for him, became the first necessary step on his road to eventual recovery.

Flight From Reality

From the ghettos of Boston to the glitter of Beverly Hills you'll find people living with deeds they won't discuss and problems they refuse to recognize. They not only lie to the world, they delude themselves. It's called denial.

- A woman who has been diagnosed with breast cancer is unable to face the truth about her condition.
- An accountant has stolen cash from his company for so long that his conscience is seared and he no longer thinks about it.
- A teenager, raped by her step-father, is unwilling to allow the memory to surface.
- A compulsive overeater declares, "There's no link between my eating habits and pressures I may be under."
- A man serving time in prison for car theft, shrugs it off by saying, "What happened, happened. It won't affect my future."
- A former prostitute says, "I don't remember what it was like on the streets. I often think that happened to someone else."
- A chain smoker brags, "I can quit

this habit anytime I choose."

• A graphic artist who has been fired from her last three jobs, complains, "Those people just don't recognize talent when they see it."

One pattern, however, continues to emerge: The greater the problems, the greater the denial. According to Harvard professor Sisella Bok, author of *Secrets,* medical doctors find that "among seriously ill patients who learn that death is near, at least 20 percent have no memory after a few days of having received such news. Faced with intolerable anxiety, they have blocked out the information."[1]

Many people become adept at erasing their past.

"Tell me about your upbringing. What was your childhood like?" I recently asked a man who wanted to talk about a behavioral problem he was having.

"Well, I was raised in a fine home and had two parents who loved me," he began. Much later in the conversation, I realized that his initial picture of a normal, average home was a far stretch from reality. For years he refused to admit that he had been extremely abused by his father when he was a child. He confessed, "I have completely blocked out that part of my life."

When faced with the painful truth of a past event, I have heard people exclaim, "What in the world are you talking about? That happened ages ago. I'm fine. I really am." Yet their words are only a cover for the reality they desperately attempt to keep submerged.

Often it takes the safety of adulthood or a different environment for the truth to slowly surface for many victims.

I have been asked, "Richard, is there any positive role for denial? Are there times it may be necessary?"

Yes, I believe that blocking out bad news is a survival mechanism God allows to help pull us through the first days, or even years, of a dreadful ordeal or a horrible shock. But it is never designed to be a permanent strategy of coping with life. Every psychologist will tell you that victims of a traumatic experience will go through many stages on their way to recovery — mental collapse, denial, guilt, bitterness, blame, self discovery, and finally healing and restoration.

The real danger is when we choose to stay in a permanent state of denial. I've seen it happen to individuals who have gone through a divorce or have lost someone they deeply love.

I will never forget visiting a nursing home and seeing an elderly woman holding a framed photo of her husband. She was talking to him as if he were still alive. A nurse said, "Oh, she does that for hours every day. She wants to believe he is still by her side."

Tuning Out

In August 1989 I stood before the Honorable Robert Potter, chief judge of the United States District Court of Western North Carolina. The Charlotte courtroom was packed as he pronounced my sentence. I was in such a state of shock and disbelief that I did not hear — or I chose to tune out — the judge's order.

A few minutes later, driving away from the federal building with my family and two attorneys, I asked, "Will someone please tell me what my sentence is?"

"You don't know?" one of the surprised lawyers exclaimed.

"No. I really don't."

My attorney, Mark Callaway, told me that I had been sentenced to eight years in prison. Even then, the words didn't truly sink in. They seemed so foreign to me.

Later, I learned that I was to be incarcerated at Eglin Federal Prison, located at the Eglin Air Force Base near Pensacola, Florida. When people asked me about it I could not bring myself to say the word "prison." Even when I visited the facility about two months before I began serving my sentence, I called it "the camp," "the facility," or "the institution."

I was in denial until I faced my problems and confessed my sins to God and to others.

As you can imagine, I have spent countless hours analyzing my mistakes and wrestling with choices I have made. *How could I have allowed something like this to happen?* I wondered.

Did I deliberately set out to become involved in a fraud or a deceit? Absolutely not! But when you get permission from your conscience to have a small secret, then you get the green light to have an even larger secret. And that can be devastating.

Suddenly, you are in water that is over your head. On one hand you are denying the seriousness of the problem and on the other hand you are giving alibis. You intentionally shape people's opinions concerning your motives, your agenda, and your financial decisions. Because I had given my mind consent to hold dark secrets, I found it easy to shade the truth about my salary, the purpose of trips I was taking, and the reasons for my meetings with attorneys.

I have asked myself a thousand times, *Why didn't*

I just say "No" to the first secret I was asked to harbor? I should have listened to my heart.

Partial Details

I've learned from experience that some people, even after receiving the most professional counseling, do not find relief from their problem. Why? Because there is often an important part of the puzzle that is missing — a vital link of information the person refuses to share.

I recall the time a couple who owned a small restaurant came to my office. It was the wife who made the appointment and I could tell immediately that her husband didn't want to be there. "Pastor Dortch," she began, "something has happened to our marriage and I don't know what's gone wrong."

In the course of two meetings with the couple, the husband's hostility seemed to soften. They began to open up and address their faults. At the end of the second session they left smiling, determined to give their marriage a fresh start.

One year later, I had an urgent call from the woman. She was crying as she told me that she was filing for divorce that same day.

"What has happened?" I wanted to know.

"He was not honest with me, or with you," she responded. "I learned that for the past three years he has had an ongoing affair with one of the waitresses who works for us. I couldn't believe it but he confessed that it's true."

Without total honesty and transparency, life is only a charade. If we attempt to conceal or evade responsibility for sin, we practice self-deceit and contribute to our own demise, both physically and spiritually. "He who covers his sins will not prosper, but whoever confesses and forsakes them will have mercy" (Prov. 28:13).

Five Steps Out of Denial

How can we break free from being caught in a web of secrecy and self-deception? Here are five helpful steps.

1. Face the facts.

Your dilemmas won't disappear because you refuse to acknowledge them. Being raised on a farm I know what happens when you ignore the small worms in a few ears of corn or the weeds growing in a strawberry patch. If you fail to rectify the problem the entire crop will be ruined.

Instead of playing mental tricks on yourself or pretending the matter doesn't exist, bring the issue to the surface. Let me suggest that you take a piece of paper and a pen and write a statement to yourself that includes all of the facts. Next, write down what you are going to do about it. Then read it to yourself and sign it.

One man not only wrote such a letter but he put a stamp on it and mailed it to himself. A few days later he opened the envelope and read again what he had written. He said, "I was more determined than ever to conquer the situation."

2. Realize that nothing can be totally hidden.

One of the first lessons I learned in childhood was this: "You can run, but you can't hide." It was the story of Jonah and the whale.

It's easy to deceive your business associates, your friends, and even your family. It's more difficult to deceive yourself. It is totally impossible, however, to hide anything from God. As the writer of Hebrews declared, "There is no creature hidden from His sight, but all things are naked and open to the eyes of Him to whom we must give account" (Heb. 4:13).

God not only knows every intimate detail of our faults and failures, He has provided a means for the slate to be wiped clean. His only requirement is that we recognize our need, confess our sins, and receive His forgiveness. It begins with being totally honest before Him.

3. When the Lord speaks, listen!

A man in Norfolk, Virginia, informed me about what he planned to do to escape from the predicament he was in. After listening for a few moments, I asked this simple question. "I know about *your* plans, but what strategy has the Lord given you?"

It was a question he hadn't expected. "Oh, the Lord's got enough problems," he exclaimed. "He's given me the intelligence to handle this on my own."

Placing my hand on his shoulder, I said, "Sir, I think we need to pray."

I believe God erects warning signs along our path for a purpose. He want us to pause long enough so that He can offer supernatural advice.

We are not lost in a never-ending maze. He is calling: "Follow My direction. Here's the way out." Listen to your heart.

4. Surrender to the truth.

Every time I pass the checkout stand at the grocery story I'm astonished at the headlines on the tabloid newspapers. "Instant Cure for Arthritis." "The Amazing Five-Minute Diet." "Science Discovers Muscle-Building Pill."

People are looking for quick-as-lightning answers to their deep-seated problems. They will try almost anything to avoid the discipline that is often necessary to see their difficulty solved.

Our answer will not arrive until we surrender ourselves to the truth and all of its implications. God's timetable may be as fast as the twinkling of an eye. Or He may have a plan that requires a lifetime of discipline.

Don't be sidetracked by answers that are not based in reality. Look for truth, recognize truth, and submit yourself to it.

The only denial the Lord allows is *self-denial*. Jesus says, "If any may follow me, let him deny himself and take up his cross and follow me" (Mark 8:34).

5. Open the windows of your heart.

When I moved to Florida there was something I immediately noticed. No matter how sweltering it is during the day, at night you can expect to feel a refreshing breeze — an experience you'll miss if your windows are tightly closed.

Those who continue to live in a state of denial eventually find themselves in an oppressive and confining atmosphere. They are not only bound by their secret, but are plagued by a growing list of predicaments. They suffer from a lack of spiritual oxygen.

If you are bound by self-deception or refuse to accept the truth, let me urge you to take the steps we've outlined. Let God help you remove the clouds that threaten your life. You'll feel the fresh, clear breeze of peace in your heart. Open the window and allow it to come in.

10

"I Have a Confession"

*"Confess your sins to each other
and pray for each other so that you may
be healed"* (James 5:16).

At Grand Central Station in the heart of New York City a commuter was waiting for his train to Long Island. About two minutes later a stranger sat down next to him and struck up a conversation.

"It's been a rough day for me," the stranger began. Immediately he started talking about the mountain of problems that had been troubling his life. Like a torrent of muddy water spilling over a dam the man spewed out details of how his marriage was on the rocks, how his children had forsaken him and his wife, and how he was on the verge of being fired from his job.

The commuter patiently listened as the stranger poured out his heart about his personal failures. It was more than an hour later before the man finally stood to his feet and said, "Sir, you'll never know what this has meant to me to share this with a person who would listen. I had to tell somebody." Then, the stranger disappeared off into the night.

The man who had been listening didn't take the train to Long Island. Instead he went back to his office in Manhattan where he was a journalist. At his computer keyboard he began to write about the need for a safe haven where people could find someone — anyone — to share the deepest secrets of their soul.

Can We Talk?

Today, it seems we live in a world of strangers. No longer can we chat with the owners of the corner grocery store or the mechanic at the local service station. We now have giant supermarkets and pump our own gas.

Front porches have disappeared from our homes and with our hectic schedules we don't have time to really get to know our neighbors.

I am gravely concerned about a generation of children whose major discussion with their parents concerns what television channel they will turn to that evening.

For several years I have hosted a TV program called "You and Me." It is a live two-hour call-in telecast that is seen in the middle of the night. People phone in from all parts of the nation and we pray with them concerning issues they are facing.

One of the most phenomenal things about the program is that we receive a large number of calls from children — 10, 11, 12, and 13 years old.

"Why is this happening?" I asked my producer. "Why are these kids calling at this hour of the night?"

He replied, "Children these days don't have anybody to talk with and you are like a substitute parent; a father figure to them. They feel free to talk with you because you are there. You listen. And you treat them with respect."

Every person — children included — needs a special someone to whom they can bare their heart.

Who Should We Tell?

The process we are discussing is not a new one. In Scripture we can find distinct guidelines for admitting our faults. There are also clear parameters of how problems between Christians are to be dealt with. In some situations, confession is called for. In others, a person is to be confronted in their transgression.

For example, if a person feels he or she has been wronged, they are to go directly to the offending party and earnestly seek a resolution of the conflict (Matt. 18:15).

What happens if the one who has offended refuses to listen to the person confronting them? Then two or three are to face the offender (Matt. 18:16). If the matter is still unresolved it is to be brought before the church in a public forum (Matt. 18:17). As the writer of the Book of Proverbs says, though a person's hatred "is covered by deceit, his wickedness will be revealed before the whole congregation" (Prov. 26:26).

The objective is forgiveness and restoration.

I become worried when I hear about a person or a ministry that does not come under the discipline and accountability of a local church or religious body. There are built-in safeguards in the system God has established.

Unfortunately, there are some congregations who carry the issue of confession too far. They conduct meetings where members are urged to reveal virtually every thought and deed of their private life. This is a dangerous practice.

Making it Right

If there is a personal issue that involves only you, and the matter can be solved directly between you and the Lord, do it. The sin of pornography is a good example. If God gives deliverance to the man or woman who has an addiction to sexually explicit literature, there is no valid reason to stand before a congregation and confess it.

When should a personal sin become a matter to be handled in confidence with someone else? Only when the troubling behavior persists. Accountability to another person gives the motivation necessary to resist the sinful act. Your conscience will give you the signal you need to ask for help.

If we have harmed another individual in any way, we need to make it right with them. There is something within us that cannot find peace until such a matter is resolved.

I was recently asked, "Richard, what do you think about those in some churches who confess their sins to a priest?"

My answer surprised them. I said, "When it comes to the confessional, Protestants have thrown out the baby with the bath water. There is a place for unburdening our hearts to another human as well as to God.

We've denied many people that important process."

Don't misunderstand me. I know that Scripture tells us that no man comes to God except through the Son. But the same Bible tells us that we are to confess our sins one to another (James 5:16).

I have spent a lifetime praying with people at an altar. I've heard them say, "God, forgive me of my sins." At those moments I have rejoiced and said to them, "You are forgiven."

Because of the code of conduct adhered to by counselors, the client can expect that the details of their conversations will be strictly private. But there are exceptions, even for professionals.

The moment a person says to me, "Can I talk to you in confidence?" I let them know that there are certain things a counselor is bound by law to share with authorities. For example:

1. If the person plans to harm himself.
2. If the person already has or plans to harm someone else.
3. If the person is or has been involved in child molestation.

He Couldn't Sleep

It was five o'clock in the morning when the telephone awakened me from a deep sleep. In the darkness I reached for the phone receiver on the night stand next to my bed and heard a troubled, broken voice.

"Pastor Dortch," a man said through his tears, "I must see you immediately." It was someone I knew quite well.

"How long will it take you to get here?" I asked.

"I can be there in about two hours," he told me.

At seven o'clock that morning I was waiting in my office when the man walked in. He was sobbing so deeply that his entire body was shaking. It took several minutes to calm him to the point that he could tell me why he was so distraught.

Finally, through his grief he began to share with me about the shameful sin he had participated in the night before. After being used of God for many years and living a blameless life, he had made a horrible mistake. For the first time in his life, he committed an act of adultery. It happened just a few hours before our meeting.

"In over 20 years of married life," he told me, "my wife has never thanked me or complimented me for anything that has ever happened in our ministry together." He then proceeded to tell me about a woman who was the Sunday school superintendent at his church who constantly showered him with praise for his messages, his leadership, and what his ministry meant to her.

Then he cried, "Last night I compromised my whole life. In a moment of weakness I yielded to temptation. I am in hell! Pastor Dortch, I confessed to my wife this morning and now I am here to face the consequences for my actions."

His mistake was costly to his family and ministry, but he was able to put his life back together much more quickly because of the immediate action he took.

In the United States, by law, a person who is charged with an offense is guaranteed a speedy trial. Why? Because the events are still fresh in everybody's mind. And the sooner a person can deal with their problem, the quicker they will be free from it. That same rule needs to apply to our personal confession.

Making Decisions

I enjoy the game of baseball and am especially fond of *my* team, the Saint Louis Cardinals. I remember the day at the stadium when I said to myself, "That's Babe Ruth over there. He's one of the best to ever play the game." I also remember watching Joe DiMaggio, Ted Williams, Hank Aaron, Mickey Mantle, and Willie Mays when they came to town.

You couldn't have a game, however, without an umpire. Many important conflicts are only resolved with the aid of an umpire.

Do you realize that we have an internal built-in arbitration that helps guide our decisions? Paul wrote that we should "let the peace of God rule in your hearts" (Col. 3:15). The word rule is translated "umpire."

I was once asked by a member of my staff, "How can I know what information I should be sharing with you?"

"When in doubt, tell me," I responded.

The same rule applies to the question, "Shall I repent? Do I need to confess this transgression?" If there is the slightest doubt, do it!

A Troubled Heart

It was Friday night and I was delivering a message to a large conference on the West Coast. As part of my remarks I made this statement: "We thunder to our kids 'Don't steal,' and yet they watch us sneak things home from our workplace."

The next morning, during a break in a seminar I

was presenting to the same group, a man pulled me aside and said, "Reverend Dortch, I have been an officer in a church for over 11 years and I took an item from my job that is so big I don't know how to get it back. I can't sleep. I have not rested since 8:30 last night when you said what you did."

I asked, "What is the value of the item?"

"It's worth over $7,200 and I could never come up with that kind of money," he told me. Then he suggested a way out of his dilemma. "What if I arrange to return the item and not let anyone know I have taken it?"

"That won't help," I said. "You'd still be guilty of deception. This matter needs to be handled openly." I knew he had to face up to his failure. The problem was resolved when I took him to his pastor where he asked forgiveness and agreed to make restitution.

Long ago, God told Moses to tell the people, "When a man or woman wrongs another in any way and so is unfaithful to the Lord, that person is guilty and must confess the sin he has committed. He must make full restitution for wrong." (Num. 5:6-7;NIV). Even more, they were instructed to add one-fifth of the value and give it all to the person who had been wronged (Num. 5:8).

Release from Guilt

I recently received a letter from a woman who had just finished reading my book, *Integrity*. She wrote, "I have lived with guilt because of something I did several years ago. I was involved in shoplifting at three different department stores." After becoming a Christian she realized she had to face her secrets.

She explained, "Even though those stores had

been sold and had new owners I felt I had to do some-thing to make things right." After reading my book and talking to her pastor, she made the trek to each of the three establishments, making amends for the things she had taken.

She said, "I couldn't believe how understanding and supportive the executives of those firms were. Yet that is incidental. I finally felt God's peace in my heart."

Recently, after a speaking engagement, I was ap-proached by a father who introduced me to his son — a young man in his thirties. "Pastor Dortch, my son has had a terrible failure in his life. He has made some unwise judgments and horrible mistakes."

I could sense there was much more to the story than they were telling and I did something that was quite unusual for me. I looked at the young man and felt led to ask, "How much money did you take from your company?"

The two men looked at each other in disbelief. Then the son admitted that he had taken thousands of dollars over a long period of time before he was ex-posed and fired from the firm.

When he was caught, management told him, "If you had voluntarily come to us and admitted the fact that you had done this, and offered to make it right, we would have given you a second chance. Now that is impossible." The penalty was full restitution and the loss of a career at the firm.

I believe his employer made a wise decision.

While I was having coffee with a group of busi-nessmen, I was asked a hypothetical question. "What if a man who has committed 10 murders suddenly becomes a born-again Christian and asks God to forgive him? Does the man have an obligation to confess his past to authorities?"

"Yes," I responded. "And the same is true for the person who has been a thief or a rapist." The Lord purifies our heart, but we must take legal responsibility for breaking the laws that govern society.

Cleansing is not only necessary, it is required.

Whether we confess to ourselves, to God, or to our fellow man, the process is essential. It's good for the soul!

11

Honest to God

*"Satan trembles when he sees, the
weakest saint upon his knees."*
— William Cowper

You may be able to mislead those around you,
and even deceive yourself, but regardless of how much
you try, you can never fool God. Every moment of
your life is totally known to Him.

The most honest moments you will ever experience are those spent alone with God in prayer.

I remember the day I was in a hospital bed, about
to undergo my second surgery in less than one week.
My kidney was going to be removed and the situation
was life-threatening. Mildred had been by my side,
but she was asked to go to the waiting room. Now it
was just me and the Lord and I bared my soul before
Him.

Several months after I became a federal inmate I
was suffering with a hernia that had torn loose and

required immediate surgery. It was January 1991. As three doctors at Eglin Air Force Hospital were examining me the night before the operation, the Chief of Internal Medicine asked, "Do you know why your ankles are swollen?"

"I'm not sure," I responded, "but I have noticed the condition for some time and I have been very concerned about it."

He said, "I'd like to do a CAT scan after this surgery."

The delicate operation for the hernia went extremely well and three days later I was taken to the radiology department for the CAT scan. The physicians didn't like the results. The Chief of Surgery came into my room and said, "Pastor Dortch, you have a large cyst on your right kidney that I feel we should keep watching. However, what deeply concerns me is that your left kidney has a mass that needs further analysis."

Immediately they sent me by ambulance to a medical facility in Fort Walton Beach, Florida, where I was placed inside a scanning chamber for a procedure known as magnetic resonance imaging (MRI).

When I returned to the Air Force hospital the surgeon came to my bedside and gave me the dreaded news. "I'm sorry to tell you this," he said, "but the tests show that you have cancer and we have to remove your left kidney as soon as we can arrange it."

The word "cancer" triggered shock waves of fear. My ministry had collapsed. I was in prison. And now this. I wondered, "Is there anything else that could possibly go wrong?"

Under the Bridge

It was early in the morning when the hospital assistants came to wheel me to the operating room. I realized that no one could have this surgery for me, and I have never felt so alone.

It is our nature to run to someone for help, but that morning I didn't have that option.

As they pushed my bed down the hall, I remember going through the double-wide framed doorway into the surgery room. When I passed under that frame it was as if I were going under a bridge. I breathed up a prayer and said, "Lord you have always been faithful. I abandon myself totally to you."

At that moment I also remember praying, "Lord, I know that you have a plan and a destiny for my life. Please show me what it is." I then resigned myself from every aspiration and dream that I desired for my future. From the depths of my soul, I prayed, "Father, not my will, but Thy will be done."

I looked up to heaven and said, "I'm ready today. If that means death — or if it means life." I realized this was one more trial I must go through and it was a lonely one. The television cameras were not on. There was no podium, and no audience. This wasn't being played out before the grandstands.

If faith doesn't work in private it will never work in public. If I cannot find an answer when I am alone with God, then I will never find an answer.

The operation was a success. The kidney with the cancerous growth was removed.

You're Not Alone

Don't despise the times you find yourself alone.

Jesus was led by the Spirit into the wilderness for 40 days and 40 nights. He was lonely, weary, and hungry. It was there He was tempted by Satan, but emerged victorious — ready to begin His public ministry.

For many people, however, moments of solitude become a prelude to disaster. They don't know how to deal with the temptations that come when no one else is present. As a man I counseled recently told me, "When I am alone I find myself doing things I would never do if one of my friends were with me." Then he confessed, "I made a horrible mistake because I was lonely and looked for someone to comfort me."

There is no need to turn to the world for contentment. Jesus said, "I will not leave you comfortless: I will come to you" (John 14:18).

Do you know what it means to get alone with God — to have a secret place of prayer?

Here is what Jesus said in His sermon on the Mount of Olives: "And when you pray, you shall not be like the hypocrites. For they love to pray standing in the synagogues and on the corners of the streets, that they may be seen by men. Assuredly, I say to you, they have their reward. But you, when you pray, go into your room, and when you have shut your door, pray to your Father who is in the secret place; and your Father who sees in secret will reward you openly" (Matt. 6:5-6).

Every day we are being bombarded by a relentless stream of distractions — uninvited telephone calls, news bulletins, and people begging for our attention. To make room for God, we literally have to shut out the world. Andrew Murray said, "Dwell much in the inner chamber, with the door shut — shut in from men, shut up with God; it is there the Father waits for you, it is there Jesus will teach you to pray. To be alone in secret with the Father: this be your highest joy."

Eight Keys to Prayer

With God, prayer is not an option. He *expects* you to call on Him. The Lord didn't say, "If you pray," He said, "*When* you pray" (Matt. 6:6).

How should we call on God? Here are eight important keys that will unlock the door of prayer:

1. Pray as a child of God.

As a Christian you have a personal relationship with God. He is not "the" Father, but "our" Father. That is why Jesus, when He taught us how to pray, began with the words, "Our Father, which art in heaven" (Matt. 6:9).

How are we adopted into God's family? "But as many as received Him, to them He gave the right to become children of God, even to those who believe in His name: who were born, not of blood, nor of the will of the flesh, nor of the will of man, but of God" (John 1:12,13).

Our prayers are not directed to a distant God in a far-off land. We're part of God's household of faith. He says, "I will be a Father to you, and you shall be My sons and daughters" (2 Cor. 6:18).

2. Pray with reliance on the Almighty.

The power of our prayers will never be the result of our piety, our contrition, or our righteousness. We can never rely on our strength, but on His omnipotence.

There's a time to pray, and a time to stand on the authority of God. When the children of Israel were about to be pushed into the Red Sea by Pharaoh's mighty armies, Moses cried out to the Lord, and God replied, "Why do you cry to Me? Tell the children of Israel to go forward" (Exod. 14:15). He said, "Lift up your rod, and stretch out your hand over the sea and divide it. And the children of Israel shall go on dry ground through the midst of the sea" (Exod. 14:16).

The God we serve has all things in His control. Even before we ask, the answer is on the way. "For your Father knows the things you have need of before you ask Him" (Matt. 6:8).

3. Pray with the right motives.

Why do we pray? Do we sincerely desire to build a relationship with our Heavenly Father, or are we attempting to accumulate material possessions? Jesus said, "Do not lay up for yourselves treasures on earth, where moth and rust destroy and where thieves break in and steal; but lay up for yourselves treasures in heaven, where neither moth nor rust destroys and where thieves do not break in and steal" (Matt. 6:19-20). Then He added, "For where your treasure is, there your heart will be also" (Matt. 6:21).

Examine your soul and spirit. There is no room for selfish motives in God's kingdom.

4. Pray with a clean heart.

If you expect to secure God's attention, be certain you speak from a heart that is pure. "The Lord is far from the wicked, but He hears the prayer of the righteous" (Prov. 15:29).

The Psalmist wrote, "If I regard iniquity in my heart, The Lord will not hear" (Ps. 66:18).

Prayer is meaningless unless it comes from deep within. As Charles Spurgeon observed, "The prayer of the heart is the heart of prayer."

You can rest assured that you are communicating from your heart when it is the Holy Spirit that is praying. As Paul wrote, "And because you are sons, God has sent forth the Spirit of His Son into your hearts, crying out, 'Abba, Father!' " (Gal. 4:6).

5. Pray with a forgiving spirit.

God has given us a wonderful promise. When we forgive, He will do the same. "If you forgive men their trespasses, your heavenly Father will also forgive you" (Matt. 6:14).

Because of the mistakes of my life, I have gone the second mile to ask forgiveness of those I have harmed.

Recently, after speaking at a meeting in Virginia, a man asked me, "How can we know we have truly forgiven?"

"Sir," I told him, "you will know that you have done your part when you have no more feelings of retribution or retaliation. What happened in the past may continue to cause pain and sorrow, but it no longer controls your attitudes or actions — it ceases to govern your behavior."

Jesus said: "And whenever you stand praying, if you have anything against anyone, forgive him, that your Father in heaven may also forgive you your trespasses. But if you do not forgive, neither will your Father in heaven forgive your trespasses" (Mark 11:25-26).

6. Pray with expectation.

I'll never forget the conversation I had with the minister of a rather liberal church. He told me, "Richard, I believe in prayer, but I don't expect God to answer. He has His own agenda."

"That's not the conclusion I have reached," I responded. "My Bible tells me to ask in faith and belief."

Here is what Christ emphatically declared:

> "Therefore I say to you, whatever
> things you ask when you pray, believe
> that you receive them, and you will have
> them" (Mark 11:24).

Did He say that "some" things are possible? No. Christ said "If you can believe, all things are possible to him who believes" (Mark 9:23).

Gigantic faith is not required. "If you have faith as a mustard seed, you will say to this mountain, 'Move from here to there,' and it will move; and nothing will be impossible for you" (Matt. 17:20).

What is the source of your hope? "My soul, wait silently for God alone, For my expectation is from Him" (Ps. 62:5).

7. Pray in truth.

What is the difference between true prayer and false prayer? According to what Christ said about the hypocrites in the synagogue (Matt. 6:5), the first is seen by God and has great value; the second is seen by men and is useless.

God requires honesty, sincerity, and integrity. "The Lord is near to all who call upon Him, To all who call upon Him in truth" (Ps. 145:18).

8. Pray until there is an answer.

I've met people who believe you should only pray for something once. They say, "God hears us the first time and He warns us against using 'vain repetitions' " (Matt. 6:7).

The Lord isn't against repetition, He is against

"vain" repetition. In the Garden of Gethsemane, the Bible says Christ "went away again a second time and prayed, saying, 'O My Father, if this cup cannot pass away from Me unless I drink it, Your will be done' " (Matt. 26:42). The disciples, however, were sleeping. "So He left them, went away again, and prayed the third time, saying the same words" (Matt. 26:44).

The prophet Daniel prayed a stirring prayer, but there didn't seem to be an answer. Five days passed, then 10, and even 20. He could have given up, but he didn't. Daniel "was mourning three full weeks" (Dan. 10:2).

Then, on the twenty-first day an angel arrived with the answer. What caused the delay? God heard his words on the first day (Dan 10:12). But the angel who came with the answer was delayed by the forces of Satan. It was Daniel's continuous fervent prayer that removed the hindering spirit.

Never, never cease praying. The answer will surely come.

It's Beginning to Rain

Prayer will not only give you power and provision, it will give you a reason for praise. As Richard Foster wrote, "The love of the Father is like a sudden rain shower that will pour forth when you least expect it, catching you up into wonder and praise and unspeakable speech. When this happens, do not put up an umbrella to protect yourself but rather stand in the drenching rain of the Father."[1]

The choices we make in secret not only tell us who we really are, but hold the key to God's blessing.

Recently, while driving to the television studio for my late night program, I was turning the dial on the car radio. There were scores of stations to which I could listen, I had to make a choice. Did I want to be entertained? Or did I want to be ministered to and commune with God on my way to the program?

Immediately I turned to an inspirational station and was blessed beyond words by a song that has always meant a great deal to me:

> Friendship with Jesus,
> Fellowship divine.
> Oh, what blessed sweet communion,
> Jesus is a friend of mine.[1]

I began to sing along and my car became a sanctuary. God not only touched me there, but an unusual anointing rested on the television program that night.

Prayer is a choice. Find a place to get alone with God and be totally honest with Him.

12

The Truth about Truth

"The truth is incontrovertible.
Malice may attack it, ignorance may
deride it, but in the end, there it is."
— Winston Churchill

The world's libraries are filled with volumes that document man's relentless search for truth. From Confucius to Caesar, from Muhammad to Marx, there has been a never-ending attempt by man to capture reality and claim it for his own. The search for truth continues.

Philosophers search for it through logic.
Scholars search for it through wisdom.
Scientists search for it through measurement.
Psychologists search for it through emotions.
Mystics search for it through meditation.

For many, the questions still remain, "What is truth? And where can I find it?"

My friend, there is only one source of reality. It is found in the pages of God's inspired Word! The Lord didn't come to tell us *about* truth; He *is* truth.

Here are specific things Scripture tells us about truth. Read each verse carefully and allow it to be absorbed into your spirit.

God is truth.

Moses described the Almighty by saying: "He is the Rock, His work is perfect; for all His ways are justice, a God of truth and without injustice; righteous and upright is He" (Deut. 32:4).

Christ is truth.

Jesus declared: "I am the way, the truth, and the life. No one comes to the Father except through Me" (John 14:6).

The Holy Spirit is truth.

Before Christ returned to heaven, He said, "I will pray the Father, and He will give you another Helper, that He may abide with you forever, even the Spirit of truth" (John 14:16-17).

God's Word is truth.

When the Lord prayed for believers, He asked God to: "Sanctify them by Your truth. Your word is truth" (John 17:17).

God spoke to the prophet Daniel: "But I will tell you what is noted in the Scripture of Truth" (Dan. 10:21).

The Gospel is truth.

The apostle Paul defended the message of Christ "that the truth of the gospel might continue with you" (Gal. 2:5).

God's law is truth.

The Psalmist proclaimed, "Your righteousness is an everlasting righteousness, And Your law is truth" (Ps. 119:142).

God's commandments are truth.

"You are near, O Lord, And all Your commandments are truth" (Ps. 119:151).

God's church is truth.

In Paul's letter to Timothy, he said, "I write so that you may know how you ought to conduct yourself in the house of God, which is the church of the living God, the pillar and ground of the truth" (1 Tim. 3:15).

God's ways are truth.

In John's revelation, he saw angels singing, "Great and marvelous are Your works, Lord God Almighty! Just and true are Your ways, O King of the saints!" (Rev. 15:3).

God's sayings are truth.

God instructed John to write: " 'Blessed are those who are called to the marriage supper of the Lamb!' And he said to me, 'These are the true sayings of God' " (Rev. 19:9).

God's record is truth.

The Lord answered His critics by saying, "My witness is true: for I know where I came, and where I am going (John 8:14).

God's witness is truth.

John was inspired to write: "These things says the Amen, the Faithful and True Witness, the Beginning of the creation of God" (Rev. 3:14).

God's judgment is truth.

John the Revelator heard a voice saying, "Even

so, Lord God Almighty, true and righteous are Your judgments" (Rev. 16:7).

God's light is truth.

A new commandment was given to us by John which "is true in Him and in you, because the darkness is passing away, and the true light is already shining" (1 John 2:8).

God's heavenly bread is truth.

Speaking to His followers at the Sea of Galilee, Jesus said, "Most assuredly, I say to you, Moses did not give you the bread from heaven, but My Father gives you the true bread from heaven" (John 6:32).

God's vine is truth.

The Lord told the disciples, "I am the true vine, and My Father is the vinedresser" (John 15:1).

God's holiness is truth.

Scripture tell us to "Put on the new man which was created according to God, in righteousness and true holiness" (Eph. 4:24).

God's tabernacle is truth.

The writer of Hebrews describes "the true tabernacle which the Lord erected, and not man" (Heb. 8:2).

God's grace is truth.

Peter declared that "this is the true grace of God in which you stand" (1 Pet. 5:12).

Truth brings freedom.

Jesus boldly told the world, "And you shall know the truth, and the truth shall make you free" (John 8:32).

Truth brings growth.

Paul encouraged the church at Ephesus not to be tossed about, but rather "speaking the truth in love, (you) may grow up in all things into Him who is the head; Christ" (Eph. 4:15).

Truth brings knowledge.

In his letter to Timothy, Paul wrote that God desires that "all men to be saved and to come to the knowledge of the truth" (1 Tim. 2:4).

Truth brings the Lord near.

The Psalmist declared: "The Lord is near to all who call upon Him, To all who call upon Him in truth" (Ps. 145:18).

Truth brings love.

John wrote his third epistle to an elder in the church, "whom I love in truth" (3 John 1:1).

Truth is to be obeyed.

The Lord promises "eternal life to those who by patient continuance in doing good seek for glory, honor, and immortality; but to those who are self-seeking and do not obey the truth, but obey unrighteousness; (there will be) indignation and wrath, tribulation and anguish" (Rom. 2:7-9).

Truth is precious.

"Buy the truth, and do not sell it, also wisdom and instruction and understanding" (Pro. 23:23).

Truth preserves us.

The Lord provides a way for us to be sustained and upheld. The Psalmist prayed, "Do not withhold Your tender mercies from me, O Lord; Let Your lovingkindness and Your truth continually preserve me" (Ps. 40:11).

Truth purifies us.

Peter declared, "Since you have purified your souls in obeying the truth through the Spirit in sincere love of the brethren, love one another fervently with a pure heart" (1 Pet. 1:22).

Truth brings the new birth.

What brings us to salvation? "In Him you also trusted, after you heard the word of truth, the gospel of your salvation; in whom also, having believed, you were sealed with the Holy Spirit of promise" (Eph. 1:13).

Truth brings sanctification.

Christ prayed, "Sanctify them by Your truth. Your word is truth. . . . And for their sakes I sanctify Myself, that they also may be sanctified by the truth" (John 17:17,19).

Truth is your shield.

We have been given this promise: "Surely He shall deliver you from the snare of the fowler; And from the perilous pestilence. His truth shall be your shield and buckler" (Ps. 91:3-4).

Truth brings strength and protection.

When we put on the armor of God we are to " Stand therefore, having girded your waist with truth, having put on the breastplate of righteousness" (Eph. 6:14).

We are to walk in truth.

John wrote: "For I rejoiced greatly when brethren came and testified of the truth that is in you, just as you walk in the truth. I have no greater joy than to hear that my children walk in truth" (3 John 1:3-4).

We are to speak in truth.

What should be the guiding principle of our words? Paul declared, "For if in anything I have boasted to him about you, I am not ashamed. But as we spoke all things to you in truth, even so our boasting to Titus was found true" (2 Cor. 7:14).

Truth is eternal.

"For the Lord is good; His mercy is everlasting; And His truth endures to all generations" (Ps. 100:5).

From Genesis (Gen 42:16) to Revelation we discover that "These words are faithful and true" (Rev. 22:6). Receive them with an open mind, a willing heart and a loving spirit. In the words of writer John Hus:

> *See the truth.*
> *Listen to the truth.*
> *Teach the truth.*
> *Love the truth,*
> *Abide by the truth,*
> *And defend the truth.*
> *Until Death.*[1]

13

Keeping Your Principles in a Permissive World

*"To keep your secret is wisdom,
but to expect others to keep it is folly."*
— Samuel Johnson, English author

Hundreds of evangelical organizations were in shock. Some were on the brink of financial collapse. Could it be possible that they had been hoodwinked out of large sums of money by an unscrupulous man who had gained their confidence and trust?

In May 1995, the Securities and Exchange Commission sued John G. Bennett Jr. and his Philadelphia-based Foundation for New Era Philanthropy. They accused him of engaging in a "massive" fraud that cheated a large number of well-respected charitable institutions and some of the nation's wealthiest financiers.

The proposal was simple. According to a front page story in the *Wall Street Journal,* "Donors handed over money to the foundation which, in turn, promised to match their gifts with funds obtained from other anonymous donors. Mr. Bennett said the entire amount would then be turned over to charitable institutions."[1]

The SEC charged it was a Ponzi scheme where victims are repaid for a period of time from other victims' money until no one can be found to put up fresh capital. Early investors in New Era doubled their money and the word spread. When it filed for bankruptcy protection, the estimate was that New Era owed as much as $500 million to hundreds of groups and individuals — from Wheaton College to Laurance Rockefeller. The list of investors looks like a "who's who" among evangelical organizations — Moody Bible Institute, Youth for Christ, World Vision, etc.

The question people asked was, "Why did so many intelligent people entrust Mr. Bennett with so much money?" Tony Carnes, vice president of a nonprofit research group who became suspicious of the double-your-money scheme and asked state and federal officials to investigate New Era, described the good people who were throwing their money at the organization. "They could just taste the money," he said. "I've never seen anything like it. The weakness around the mouth, the desire in the eyes. I've always heard the expression, 'You can see greed written,' but I've seen the reality."[2]

Finally, Bennett admitted to his staff that there

were no anonymous donors. Both New Era and Bennett were sued by the SEC for alleged securities-law violations.

An Erosion of Ethics

There is a worldwide crisis of ethics that affects every level of society — rich and poor, young and old, Christian and non-Christian.

People don't keep their word. That is why major airlines overbook their flights by as much as 20 percent.

At the wedding altar, couples make a solemn vow to never part until death — yet 50 percent of all marriages will end in divorce. What good was their vow?

Things we once believed to be confidential are now being shared with the world. The "Information Highway" has made our secrets public. Data we once believed to be confidential is now being shared by tax authorities, banks, credit bureaus, school officials, corporations, insurance companies, and medical professionals. Unfortunately, much of that information can be easily obtained by your next door neighbor with nothing more than a computer and a modem. The walls of secrecy have been cracked and are rapidly eroding. For example, a school guidance counselor can browse through psychiatric records to determine the emotional stability of the family of a student.

A confused public is demanding laws of confidentiality and laws of revelation at the same time. The duplicity has raised more questions than it has solved.

The confidentiality crisis must not be seen as just a problem of society. It is personal and affects ordinary people like you and me.

After I recently addressed a trade association on the West Coast, one of the executives of the group asked to speak to me privately.

We had only been together for a few minutes when the secrets he was harboring began to flow out of him like a river. "My job requires me to hold confidences very close and to sit in judgment of others," he told me. "But now I am involved in a situation that could break at any moment and ruin my life."

In my crisis counseling, I have learned that the problems people face are usually much, much larger than they first admit. A man once came to me and told me, "I have become involved in a $3 million cover-up." That wasn't half of the story. When all of the truth had been revealed, the cover-up amounted to over $11 million.

One of the great lessons I have learned in my search for integrity is that you cannot place a monetary value on a heart that is pure and a conscience that is clear. As financial counselor Larry Burkett observes, "There is little doubt that a totally honest businessman or woman will experience some losses and will be misused by others, at least in the short run. But I believe God will compensate for any losses in many ways, not the least of which is supernatural peace."[3]

Justifying the Means

Some people attempt to rationalize their unethical behavior by seeing their actions as actually helping society. They believe the end justifies the means.

In Washington, DC, a private escrow agent for the Department of Housing and Urban Development diverted as much as $5.5 million from the agency to provide food, clothing, and shelter for the poor in the nation's capitol. She bought houses and cars for the impoverished and provided funds for them to start their own businesses.

How did the woman explain it? "There were so many hurting people," she stated. "We bought them groceries. We paid their electric bills so they could be warm. We paid their rent."

The government worker saw herself as a modern-day Robin Hood, stealing from the rich to help the poor. Regardless of the "spin" the woman tried to give her actions, stealing is still stealing and she was punished for her crime.

If truth is not written on our hearts, nothing else matters. As Job asked long ago, "How then can you comfort me with empty words, since falsehood remains in your answers?" (Job 21:34).

Guilty of Pretense

There is a heavy price to pay for deception.

When the Early Church was growing rapidly, Satan was outraged. He entered into Ananias and Sapphira and their story is the first recorded sin in the life of the Church.

The man and his wife, active members of the congregation, had sold a piece of property. And with Sapphira's full knowledge, Ananias kept back part of the money that they had designated to God's work.

What was their sin? They pretended to give everything, but secretly kept back a portion for themselves. They were guilty of pretense, hypocrisy, and lying. Even more, their actions were premeditated and carefully planned. Plus, they did not confess their iniquity.

The apostle Peter said, "Ananias, why has Satan

filled your heart to lie to the Holy Spirit?" (Acts 5:3). Peter told him that he had not only lied to men, but to God. "Then Ananias, hearing these words, fell down and breathed his last. So great fear came upon all those who heard these things" (Acts 5:5).

About three hours later, his wife, not knowing what had happened, came in. Peter asked her to recount the details of the land transaction and wanted to know, "How is it that you have agreed together to test the Spirit of the Lord? Look, the feet of those who have buried your husband are at the door, and they will carry you out" (Acts 5:9).

Immediately, Sapphira also collapsed and died.

Peter's role was only to unmask their insincerity. It was God who brought judgment.

What happened to the Church after the sin of deceit was removed? There was a great revival and multitudes were added to the Kingdom (Acts 5:12-16).

Consensual Integrity

Far too often a business enterprise — or even a family — will drift into a permissive environment where no one takes responsibility. Soon deceit and secrecy become a way of life.

Allowing dishonesty to continue is just as much a sin as committing the act. It is "consensual" integrity that winks at lying and ignores unethical conduct. Here are some examples:

• What would you say if you were typing the resume of a politician and were asked to add facts you knew were false?

• How would you respond if you worked for an attorney and were asked to bill a client for three hours of work when you knew not more than 40 minutes were spent on the project?

• What would you say if you were the secretary of a minister who constantly inflates numbers concerning the size of his congregation when submitting data requested by his denomination?

Remember, we are our brother's keeper. We cannot sit idly by when we know in our heart something is terribly wrong. We need to stand and say, "Wait a minute! What is going on?"

You may say, "My future is at stake! If I confront what is wrong I'll jeopardize my job and could lose my career!"

In Columbus, Ohio, drivers on a busy highway couldn't believe their eyes. The door to an armored truck flew open and approximately one million dollars spilled out on the road. Immediately, the motorists stopped their cars and began running for the bank notes as fast as they could. They actually encouraged each other and shouted, "It's our money! It's ours. It's ours! Grab some while you can!"

Susan Terkel, writing about the incident, says, "Melvin Kiser was one of the motorists. He cheerfully gathered up $57,000. Soon though, his cheer soured as he wrestled with his conscience over keeping the money. After two hours of moral struggle (he decided) it was wrong to keep it. He turned the money in."[4]

About $900,000 of the one million was never recovered by the bank or the armored car company. People simply kept the money and admitted to nothing.

What would you have done?

Long ago, the writer of Proverbs penned these

words: "Bread gained by deceit is sweet to a man, but afterward his mouth will be filled with gravel" (Prov. 20:17).

If you were asked to place the issue of consensual sin on God's balancing scales. How would your silence be weighed?

Six Principles

What are the standards that guide your daily life? Can you name them? Have you ever written the principles down?

Mahatma Gandhi, the man who led India to freedom from England through non-violence, was guided by a principle that came from his heart and soul. "I would not kill for freedom," Gandhi stated, "but I am willing to die for it."

Here are six principles worth adopting:

1. My word is my bond.

Your reputation is based on your word. And your word is always on the line.

Mark McCormack, author of *What They Don't Teach You at Harvard Business School*, says, "If you say you will return a call the next day and you don't, that's enough to influence an entire relationship. There's no business law that says you ever have to return any phone call; just don't say you will."[5] Integrity cannot be purchased. It is something you earn every day.

2. I will never make a promise I do not intend to keep.

No one forces you to make a vow. It is something you do by choice. When that promise is made, there should be no turning back.

Moses told the children of Israel, "That which

has gone from your lips you shall keep and perform, for you voluntarily vowed to the Lord your God what you have promised with your mouth" (Deut. 23:23).

3. My vows to God are sacred.

The commitments you make to the Lord are much more than good intentions. They should be treated as sacred — whether the promise is spiritual or material.

Regarding our giving, Scripture tells us, "When you make a vow to God, do not delay to pay it; for He has no pleasure in fools. Pay what you have vowed. It is better not to vow than to vow and not pay" (Eccles. 5:4-5).

4. I will always listen for God's Word of caution.

The Almighty created you with a moral compass that instinctively lets you know what is right and wrong, good or evil. When that is combined with the Word of God, there is no question of the direction you should take.

Have you ever heard the Holy Spirit say, "Don't do that!" It is God's yellow light of caution.

The prophet Isaiah wrote: "Your ears shall hear a word behind you, saying, 'This is the way, walk in it,' whenever you turn to the right hand or whenever you turn to the left" (Isa. 30:21).

5. I will never speak truth with evil intent.

One the greatest sins I have ever committed involved being totally honest with the facts, yet leading people to the wrong conclusion. It was a lie for which I had to ask forgiveness — from God and from my colleagues.

The English poet William Blake wrote these powerful words:

A truth that's told with bad intent,
Beats all the lies you can invent.

6. I will build all of my relationships on truth.

Strong bonds between people are not the result of written contracts or formal agreements. They are built on a foundation of confidence.

Here's the advice of the apostle Paul: "Therefore, putting away lying, each one speak truth with his neighbor, for we are members of one another" (Eph. 4:25).

Transparency is the key to mutual trust.

I like to think of integrity as a piece of glass: It is whole and complete, yet it has two sides. It is much like you and me. We have a private side and a public side. The worth of our integrity, however, is based on whether the glass is clear and transparent, or cloudy and distorted.

Regardless of the circumstances, you can build a friendship that will endure. As Charles Swindoll states, "Real integrity stays in place whether the test is adversity or prosperity."[6]

I pray that in this permissive world, you will find principles worth keeping.

14

Ten Secrets for Truthful Living

"He who dwells in the secret place of the most High, shall abide under the shadow of the Almighty" (Ps. 91:1).

One of Aesop's fables is about a shepherd boy who looked after his flock a short distance from the small community where he lived. One day he thought he would play a trick on the villagers and have some fun at their expense. So he ran toward the village crying out with all his might: "Wolf! Wolf! Come and help! The wolves are attacking my lambs!"

The people responded immediately. They left their work and ran to the field to help him. But when they arrived the boy laughed at them; there was no wolf there.

Some time later the boy repeated the prank. The villagers came running to help and again he scoffed at them.

Then one day a wolf really did break into the fold and began killing the lambs. In great fright, the boy ran for help. "Wolf! Wolf" he screamed. "There is a wolf in the flock! Help!"

The villagers, hearing his cries, thought it was another mean trick. No one paid the least attention or rose to his assistance. The shepherd boy lost all his sheep.

This is a simple but important story because it shows the plight of people who lie. Even when they tell the truth they will not be believed.

Honesty is not something to be taken lightly or to be practiced only when it is expedient or convenient. It must become our lifestyle. Truth is at the very core of our reputation, our character, and our relationship with God.

How can we build a life where deceit and hidden sins will not flourish and prosper? Here are 10 secrets for truthful living.

Secret #1: Build an honest relationship with God.

Recently a friend asked, "Richard, what was the most profound thing that happened to you during your crisis?"

I thought for a moment and replied, "I lost my ministry, but I found the Lord."

Certainly I knew the Lord before, during, and after my experience, but by losing virtually everything I possessed I discovered a new relationship with God that surpassed anything I had previously known. As a result, He totally restored my ministry.

Somehow we have come to the conclusion that what we *do* is more important than who we are. But that is not God's measuring stick. He looks at the intentions of our heart.

What would remain if your title was removed from your occupation and you no longer had your present prominence or station in life? Since that is what happened to me, let me give you this advice: *Your connection to the Almighty is more important than any status you may have attained or any position you may hold.*

Some people talk about "finding God" as if He was the one who was lost. No, the Lord will never leave you or forsake you. He is always there.

Day after day, year after year, build a strong alliance with your Heavenly Father. Keep the lines of communication open. Come to Him in prayer. Listen to His voice and praise Him with an honest heart. Remember, "God is Spirit, and those who worship Him must worship in spirit and truth" (John 4:24).

When you build your relationship with God you will be able to say, "The Lord is my helper; I will not fear" (Heb. 13:6).

Secret #2: Take total responsibility for your personal behavior.

The link between our conduct and our character is not a coincidence.

Our commitment to honesty and integrity constantly bubbles to the surface and has a direct effect on our self-esteem. Psychologist Chris Thurman of the Minirth-Meier Clinic states, "If dedication to truth characterizes our way of living, we develop stable positive feelings of worth. The moment we wrap our lives around lies, genuine feelings of self-worth are virtually impossible."[1]

In my travels I have encountered scores of people who have tried to change the world before changing themselves. Their victories were hollow and short lived. Here is what Scripture declares: "He who rules his spirit (is greater) than he who takes a city" (Prov. 16:32).

How should we conduct our lives? With "a good conscience, in all things willing to live honestly" (Heb. 13:18).

Taking total responsibility for your behavior includes both an inward decision and an outward declaration. With the writer of Proverbs, you will say, "My mouth will speak truth; wickedness is an abomination to my lips" (Prov. 8:7).

Secret #3: Examine your life.

Much too often, people are blind-sided by their mistakes. Again and again I hear these words from people I counsel: "I had no idea this was happening in my life."

We could relieve many headaches by adopting these three rules:

First: Examine your life regularly.

Don't wait for an emergency to reflect on what is happening in your life. Just as businesses operate more efficiently with consistent, systematic audits and inventories, so can we.

Regarding preparation for communion, Paul wrote, "But let a man examine himself, and so let him eat of that bread and drink of that cup" (1 Cor. 11:28). It is a process that should never end.

Second: Examine your life completely.

A troubled man recently admitted, "Richard, there are areas of my life I am totally ashamed of. I refuse to allow myself to even think about certain things."

I told him, "Sir, you'll never find complete release until you are totally honest with yourself."

Paul told the Corinthians, "Examine yourselves as to whether you are in the faith. Prove yourselves. Do you not know yourselves, that Jesus Christ is in you?" (2 Cor. 13:5).

Get alone with God and ask Him to shine His spotlight on your heart. That is what the Psalmist did. He wrote, "Examine me, O Lord, and prove me; Try my mind and my heart" (Ps. 26:2).

Third: Examine your life truthfully.

If you want to know the value of your life you can obtain four separate estimates: the world's, your loved ones, yours, and God's. There is only one appraisal, however, that counts — the one given by the Lord.

Stop attempting to use your own perspective. See yourself as the Lord sees you. Remember, you are never out of His sight. As God asked through the prophet Jeremiah, "Can anyone hide himself in secret places, so I shall not see him?" (Jer. 23:24).

Secret #4: Live a transparent life.

The window of truth should be cleaned every day so that we can see out and the world can see in.

Truth needs no excuses — in our personal lives, in business, or in the church. David Wells, professor at Gordon-Conwell Theological Seminary, in his book *No Place for Truth,* decries today's subjective evaluation of biblical teaching, personal feelings, and interpretation. He says, "Unless truth is objective, it cannot be declared to others, cannot be taught to others, cannot be required of others."[2]

The Lord wants to uncover what has been concealed. As Job declared, "He cuts out channels in the rocks, and his eye sees every precious thing. He dams up the streams from trickling; what is hidden he brings forth to light" (Job 28:10-11).

Secret #5: Allow love to govern everything you do.

St. Augustine was once asked, "What does love look like?"

He answered, "It has the hands to help others. It has the feet to hasten to the poor and needy. It has the eyes to see misery and want. It has the ears to hear the sighs and sorrows of men. That is what love looks like."

True affection that comes from the heart is the hallmark of Christianity.

As Paul wrote, "Let all that you do be done with love" (1 Cor. 16:14).

Bitterness, hatred, jealousy, and strife draw their strength from secrecy and deceit. The power of love, however, comes from truth. Paul spoke directly to the issue when he declared, "Though I speak with the tongues of men and of angels, but have not love, I have become as sounding brass or a clanging cymbal" (1 Cor. 13:1).

Secret #6: Be firm in your faith and belief.

I remember watching a news report the day after hurricane Andrew devastated south Florida. A television crew entered an area where virtually every home was flattened except one. They rushed to interview the owner of the magnificent home that was virtually untouched. The owner and his wife had stayed in the dwelling throughout the storm and he was outside tending to his flower garden.

"Tell me about your house," the newsman asked. "Why do you think it survived?"

"I built it myself," the proud owner replied. "I knew we were in a flood zone. I studied the codes and added another one-third to everything that was required." He added, "I knew this was going to be our last house and I built it to stand the test."

Our faith becomes like a rock when it is based on God's codes and His foundation for living. As the Word tell us, "Be steadfast, immovable, always abounding in the work of the Lord, knowing that your labor is not in vain in the Lord" (1 Cor. 15:58).

Have convictions and stick to them. "Be diligent to present yourself approved to God, a worker who does not need to be ashamed, rightly dividing the word of truth" (2 Tim. 2:15).

Secret #7: Commit your ways to the Lord.

The reason God uses so many different kinds of people to fulfill the Great Commission is that He reaches people where they are. Bank presidents communicate best with other bank presidents, just as truck drivers know how to reach their peers. By communicating on hundreds of different levels, the gospel becomes unavoidable.

Each of us has customs, manners, and habits that are totally unique. The question we must ask is this: Do our daily practices reflect a commitment to the Lord? Scripture tells us to "search out and examine our ways, and turn back to the Lord" (Lam. 3:40).

Every day we need to pray, "Remove from me the way of lying; And grant me Your law graciously" (Ps. 119:29).

Secret #8: Live for the good of others.

Not all secrets are bad. In fact, there is one I highly recommend. It is called "anonymous giving."

If you want to experience a sense of joy and satisfaction that goes beyond the ordinary, try doing something where there is no recognition or reward. For example, if you are in a restaurant and see a family that is obviously needy, walk over to the manager and say, "I would like to pay the check for those people over there, but please don't tell them."

That's the right kind of a secret.

Truth blossoms and grows when we stop looking at ourselves and start living for others. When self is crucified, it is almost impossible to harbor harmful secrets or deceit.

Secret #9: Dedicate yourself to truth.

Some people stretch honesty beyond the limits.

I heard about a fisherman who had his line in the water all day and didn't get as much as a nibble. Finally he headed for shore and began the drive home. On the way he stopped at a grocery store that advertised fresh fish for sale.

"Throw me a dozen of the biggest fish you have," the man said to the woman at the counter.

"Throw them? Why?" the woman asked.

"Because I'm going to catch them. I may be a lousy fisherman, but I'm not a liar."

Was he deceitful? Absolutely. He needed to pray with the Psalmist, "Deliver my soul, O Lord, from lying lips; And from a deceitful tongue" (Ps. 120:2).

God deals harshly with those who believe truth is an option. He says, "Woe to those who call evil good, and good evil; who put darkness for light, and light for darkness; who put bitter for sweet, and sweet for bitter!" (Isa. 5:20).

One of the great heroes of World War II was General George Patton. His nickname was "Old Blood and Guts." Patton was both criticized and beloved, misunderstood and honored. One thing, however, was certain. He knew how to build a winning army. Soldiers who fought alongside Patton knew this legendary warrior was a man of truth and they trusted him.

Porter B. Williamson, an officer on Patton's staff, said Patton "spoke the truth with a forceful attitude whether it was pleasant information or not." His constant command to the staff was, "Get the facts, get the truth, and get it to the troops."[3]

Dedicate yourself to truth. As Thomas Jefferson observed, "Honesty is the first chapter in the book of wisdom."

Secret #10: Develop a spirit of hope and expectation.

When I was about to be released from prison, there was a sense of excitement and anticipation that is difficult to describe. My dreams were getting bigger and my faith was soaring.

Today, when I feel my spirits sagging, I can rekindle the flame of encouragement by recalling those moments of my past.

What we envision needs to always be based on truth. As author John Burroughs wrote, "To treat your facts with imagination is one thing, to imagine your facts is another."

Ask the Lord to place a spirit of hope and expectation deep within your spirit. Ask yourself:

> Have I developed an honest relationship
>   with the Lord?
> Have I taken personal responsibility for
>   my behavior?
> Have I examined my life?
> Is my life transparent?
> Is love governing my actions?
> Am I firm in my faith, and have I committed my ways to Him?
> Am I living for others, and have I dedicated myself to truth?

The secrets for truthful living will only come alive when you embrace them with open arms and release them through action.

15

"I'm Free!"

"I pardon him, as God shall pardon me."
— William Shakespeare

I glanced at my watch. It was nine o'clock in the morning as I saw Mildred driving up to the front of the halfway house in St. Petersburg, Florida.

My heart was leaping for joy. This was the first day since my incarceration that I was totally free to do whatever I wanted for an entire day. Like a child, I jumped into the front seat of that Mercury Cougar which had about 100,000 miles on it.

When I looked at my wife who had so faithfully stood by me during my dreadful ordeal, there was a sense of release that swept over me and I began to weep. I threw up my hands and I said, "I'm free! Honey, I'm free!" And out of the depths of my spirit I shouted, "There's nothing else to come out. There's nothing left to fear. I'm free!"

I knew that there were no more secrets waiting to be revealed — no more government investigations, no more media headlines. I had told the truth and paid the price for my mistakes. Now I was free!

For years I had declared from the pulpit, "You can know what it means to be free!" I was speaking of the spiritual freedom that accompanies a born-again experience. But prison gave me an appreciation for freedom I never anticipated.

There were nights it seemed the walls were closing in so tightly I thought I would be crushed. Other times I felt an intense heaviness in my chest. Then there was the pain of shame and rejection. I was devastated being cut off from those I loved and not being able to continue my life's work. Like the Psalmist, I prayed, "O Lord; how long?" (Ps. 6:3).

When my day of freedom arrived, the sense of relief was overwhelming. I wanted to announce to the whole world, "I'm free!"

Making Things Right

Since the day I realized that I was responsible for my mistakes I have written over one thousand personal letters asking — no, *begging* — people to forgive me. It didn't even matter when one regional news magazine wrote an article about me under the headline, "The Sorriest Man in Florida."

When you make things right with God, you want to make things right with people. I was truly sorry for my transgressions.

As you can imagine, I have become acquainted with many lawyers during the last few years. I asked one of them, "What is your advice to a person who has done something wrong?"

Almost before I had the question completed, he replied, "That's easy. I advise them to tell the truth, the whole truth, and nothing but the truth as quickly as possible." Then he gave me some examples of how judges show leniency to those who admit their errors rather than waiting to be exposed at the bar of justice.

God is the ultimate judge and He operates in the same manner. The moment you realize that you have made a mistake you should immediately say two things to the Lord:

First: "Lord, I did it."

Second: "Please forgive me."

Most people resist admitting their mistakes. Yet it is the vital first step to freedom.

An Act of Forgiveness

The liberty that comes through forgiveness is priceless.

I recently received a letter from a man who had just heard me speak.

He told me about the animosity between himself and a man with whom he had worked for the past two years. There had been many ugly words between them.

The night I spoke in their city, both of the men arrived at the auditorium early. They were surprised to see each other at the meeting and politely shook hands and found their seats.

In his letter, the man wrote, "About four minutes later he came over, knelt down, and asked forgiveness from me for his behavior during the past two years. I not only accepted his apology, but I apologized, too."

The letter continued, "I wept inside. You see, the man had just been charged with two counts of sodomy and one count of sexual harassment against his nine-year-old granddaughter. He confessed that it was true and he was awaiting a prison sentence. The man admitted his faults and was seeking to make things right with those he had harmed."

Freedom not only comes as a result of asking forgiveness of others, it is the result of the freedom that comes directly from God.

I heard the story of a priest who lived in the Philippines. He had a woman in his parish who claimed she often had visions in which she talked with Jesus and He talked with her. The priest, however, was rather skeptical of her claim and decided to put her to the test.

He said to the woman, "You tell me that you actually speak directly with the Lord in your visions. Then let me ask you a favor. The next time you have one of these visions, I want you to ask Him what terrible sin your priest committed when he was a student in the seminary."

The sin the priest was thinking of was something he had done in secret — no one knew about it except him and God. This transgression created such a burden of guilt within him that he was unable to truly experience joy or peace. Because of this past failure he found it almost impossible to live in the present. He longed for forgiveness, yet never felt he could be forgiven.

The woman agreed to ask the Lord about it the next time she was in prayer and she went home.

A few days later, when she returned to the church, the priest inquired, "Well, did Jesus visit you in your dreams?"

"Oh, yes He did," the woman replied with enthusiasm.

"Did you ask Him what sin I committed in the seminary?" he questioned rather cynically.

"Yes, Reverend. I asked Him."

"And what did He say?" the priest wanted to know.

The woman calmly and quietly responded, "He said, 'I don't remember.' "

At that moment the priest realized that God, true to His Word, had forgiven and forgotten what he had done. He was free!

When God covers your sins, they are gone forever. The Psalmist wrote, "Blessed is he whose transgression is forgiven, Whose sin is covered" (Ps. 32:1).

The Source of Freedom

Forgiveness and truth are essential to freedom. Never forget the words of Christ: "You shall know the truth, and the truth shall make you free" (John 8:32).

That strong principle affects every area of life.

A newspaper reporter once asked Sam Rayburn, speaker of the United States House of Representatives, "Mr. Speaker, you see probably a hundred people a day. You tell each one, "yes," or "no," or "maybe." You are never seen taking notes on what you told them, but I have never heard of you forgetting anything you have promised them. What is your secret?

Rayburn carefully looked at his questioner and replied, "If you tell the truth the first time, you don't have to remember."

The person who embarks on a course of deceit is building the walls of his own prison. As George Bernard Shaw observed, "The liar's punishment is not in the least that he is not believed, but that he cannot believe anyone else."

There Is Hope

A friend recently asked, "Richard, since you are involved in crisis counseling, aren't you discouraged by what you see and hear?"

"No," I told him, "I'm encouraged because I have seen enough lives restored to know that there is hope in any situation."

Where there is great bondage, there can be great liberty. Yes, you can know the sweet release of freedom.

You Can Be Free of Anxiety

I have seen the Lord replace worry with peace and power. Jesus declared, "My peace I leave with you, My peace I give to you; not as the world gives do I give to you. Let not your heart be troubled, neither let it be afraid" (John 14:27).

Listen to the Psalmist as he sings, "The Lord is my light and my salvation; Whom shall I fear? The Lord is the strength of my life; Of whom shall I be afraid?" (Ps. 27:1).

You Can Be Free of Addiction

In my ministry I have encountered people who are slaves to everything from alcohol to gambling. For some people, the answer comes instantly because of a decision. For others it is an unending process. Paul wrote, "He who has begun a good work in you will complete it until the day of Jesus Christ" (Phil. 1:6).

You Can Be Free of Anger

An unruly temper is not something you have to live with. God can remove the roots of outrage and hostility.

James advised: "Let every man be swift to hear, slow to speak, slow to wrath" (James 1:19). And Paul wrote, "Be angry, and do not sin: do not let the sun go down on your wrath" (Eph. 4:26).

You Can Be Free of Compulsive Behavior

Many people want to live guilt-free lives, but they are pulled by what seems to be an invisible force to repeat acts they know will leave them with remorse. The behavior may range from over-eating to perfectionism.

There is no project too difficult for the Lord. You can say, "I can do all things through Christ who strengthens me" (Phil. 4:13).

You Can Be Free of Jealousy

Envy and resentment can be the result of events that are either real or imagined. God's Word declares "If you have bitter envy and self-seeking in your hearts, do not boast and lie against the truth" (James 3:14).

The writer of Proverbs says, "Do not let your heart envy sinners, but in the fear of the Lord continue all day long; For surely there is a hereafter, and your hope will not be cut off" (Prov. 23:17-18).

You Can Be Free of Depression

There are people whose depression is the result of a chemical imbalance and require the care of a physician. But that is the exception, not the rule. From my vantage point, people everywhere become depressed by their own actions. They dwell on negative forces until they are overcome by their emotions.

Listen to what Jesus says: "Blessed are you who hunger now, for you shall be filled. Blessed are you who weep now, for you shall laugh" (Luke 6:21).

There is an answer for depression. I love the words of the Psalmist: "Why are you cast down, O my soul? And why are you disquieted within me? Hope in God; For I shall yet praise Him; The help of my countenance and my God" (Ps. 42:11).

God tells us, "He who overcomes shall inherit all things, and I will be his God and he shall be My son" (Rev. 21:7).

You Can Be Free of Failure

"I know that because I failed once, I will surely fail again," a man from Michigan recently told me.

"That doesn't have to be the case," I assured him.

The Lord "gives power to the weak, and to those who have no might He increases strength" (Isa. 40:29). "Those who wait on the Lord shall renew their strength; they shall mount up with wings like eagles, they shall run and not be weary, they shall walk and not faint" (Isa. 40:31).

You Can Be Free of Fear

Worry is more than a drain on your energy. When you dwell on negative scenarios you actually give them life. God has a remedy for unhealthy fear. He asks you to replace it with love. "There is no fear in love; but perfect love casts out fear, because fear involves torment. But he who fears has not been made perfect in love" (1 John 4:18).

The Lord has not given us a spirit of fear, "but of power and of love and of a sound mind" (2 Tim. 1:7).

You Can Be Free of Guilt

Judgment for transgressions is swift. You are sentenced with guilt the moment the sinful act is committed. Secular counselors have a difficult time in their attempts to free a person from self-condemnation. Their advice rings hollow when compared to the freedom Christ brings. What does the Word say? "There is therefore no condemnation to them which are in Christ Jesus, who walk not after the flesh, but after the spirit" (Rom. 8:1).

Say those words to yourself out loud — again and again. "No condemnation!" "No condemnation!"

Remember, "As far as the east is from the west; So far has He removed our transgressions from us" (Ps. 103:12).

You Can Be Free of Loneliness

In our crowded world there are people everywhere who feel isolated and alone. Jesus, said, "I will never leave you nor forsake you" (Heb. 13:5).

Be comforted by the Almighty when He says, "Behold, I am with you and will keep you wherever you go . . . for I will not leave you until I have done what I have spoken to you" (Gen. 28:15).

You Can Be Free of Stress

There can be hundreds of causes of unhealthy tension — from a change in our financial state to the death of a close friend. The results can be devastating, including confusion, exhaustion, even suicidal thoughts.

The Lord tells us, "He shall call upon Me, and I will answer him; I will be with him in trouble; I will deliver him and honor him." (Ps. 91:15).

"Come to Me, all you who labor and are heavy laden, and I will give you rest" (Matt. 11:28).

Nothing Between

When God's message of truth sets you free, you will want the entire world to know. Like the Psalmist, you'll declare:

> I have proclaimed the good news
> of righteousness
> In the great congregation;
> Indeed, I do not restrain my lips,
> O Lord, You Yourself know.
> I have not hidden Your righteous-
> ness within my heart;
> I have declared Your faithfulness
> and Your salvation;
> I have not concealed Your
> lovingkindness and Your truth (Ps. 40:9-
> 10).

My father, Harry Dortch, went to be with the Lord at the age of 99. On a beautiful spring morning, as the flowers were beginning to bloom, a funeral service in his honor was held in Granite City, Illinois.

The organ began to play as a beloved friend stood to sing the words of a song that was the theme of my father's life:

> *Nothing between my soul and the Sav-*
> *iour.*
> *Naught of the world's elusive dreams.*
> *Nothing preventing the least of His fa-*
> *vor.*
> *Keep the way clear, there's nothing be-*
> *tween.*[1]

16

A New Reformation

"I can do no other."
— Martin Luther

For many years I have observed how people in places of leadership attempt to justify their secrets. Since they must appropriately keep confidences of those they serve, they mistakenly believe their personal world must also be hidden.

How do I know? From first-hand experience.

When a colleague in another large organization would call to ask, "How do you deal with this?" I knew it was a code for saying "How do I hide the truth?"

The result often becomes a conspiracy of nondisclosure. It is sad but true that many leaders in business, government, and religion confer with one another to devise ways to keep "the people" from learning the truth.

When the subject is executive compensation, the issue is not how much money a person makes, but why they want to keep the facts hidden.

Centuries ago, a German priest named Martin Luther made a declaration that God intended for the decisions of our lives to be open before God and man. Decisions were to be made personally — not dictated by others. It was a freedom that required new standards of individual integrity, ethics, and principles.

Author George Will observes that when Luther uttered the words, "I can do no other," he announced "the ascendance of private judgment — of conscience." Says Will, "The life of this driven man demonstrated that the modern notion of freedom — freedom from external restraint imposed by others — can mean submission to a hard master, one's conscience."[1]

As a society, we have drifted far from the vision of Luther and the men and women of honor and character who have followed him. As William J. Bennett states in the introduction to *The Book of Virtues*, "Today we speak about values and how important it is to 'have them,' as if they were beads on a string or marbles in a pouch."[2] He adds that morality and virtues are not something to possess, but something to *be*.

I believe the time has come for a new reformation — a reformation of integrity, honesty, honor, and truth that will permeate every area of our lives.

1. We call for a reformation of ethics in the marketplace.

Business as usual must no longer remain business as usual. Leaders in commerce need to declare their intention to set a higher standard.

- Unethical means must not be used to achieve ethical goals.
- Our word must again become our bond.
- Individuals must not be trampled in the name of progress.
- Moral transgression must not be condoned at any level on the corporate ladder.
- Truth in advertising must become more than a slogan.
- The mission statement of every business should include a commitment to the basic principles of ethics.
- Issues of integrity should be openly discussed, reviewed, and reinforced on a continuing basis.

God's Word contains not only a road map for the conduct of our personal lives, but is also a guide for the direction of our businesses. Every corporate executive needs to say with Job, "Till I die I will not put away my integrity from me" (Job 27:5).

2. We call for a reformation of secrecy in government.

The Declaration of Independence begins with the words, "We the people." It is not talking about someone else, but you and me.

Somehow, in the name of progress we have allowed our elected officials to operate as if they were members of a private club or a secret society. As citizens, our complacency can no longer continue.

With the exception of preparations for war, the operation of government should be an open book. Meetings should be announced in advance and held in public. Proposed policies and revisions of law should only be made after public input and discussion.

We are much too familiar with midnight resolutions to increase the pay of government officials, or quiet, last-minute amendments attached to popular bills that are nothing more than political payoffs.

What we are proposing goes far beyond the Freedom of Information Act. Leaders at every level need to publicly declare they will only support causes and decisions with which they can be proud to associate.

3. We call for a reformation in the disclosure of information.

Information that is personal and confidential must never be shared with another individual without our written permission. That includes medical records, internal revenue documents, insurance data, and credit reports. For example, before any private information is shared, there should be a signed statement by you on file authorizing to whom that information may be made available. Unfortunately, third party data sources are scattering information about individuals like dust in the wind. A falsehood that becomes public spreads like a roaring fire. Charles Spurgeon said, "A lie travels round the world while Truth is putting on her boots."

As individuals, we must honor the commitments we make to each other regarding matters of privacy. However, facts involving the morality of leadership are a totally different matter.

Recently I learned that the chief executive of an organization in the northern part of the United States was charged with sexual misconduct. Yet the issue was glossed over and no comprehensive investigation was made because of fear that the publicity would cause the enterprise to greatly suffer.

High officials knew the truth but kept quiet by rationalizing, "The people can't handle this." They set up their own set of facts to distort the real truth. When that happens everything has its own measuring stick — 12 inches is no longer a foot and four quarters don't add up to a dollar.

The problem was compounded when the facts were inevitably revealed, and the negative impact was far worse than if the truth had been shared when it was first discovered.

Every individual and organization needs to review the manner in which information is reported. In most cases we exaggerate our gains and ignore our losses. An international missions leader told me, "If as many people are being won to Christ as reported, the world would have been totally evangelized long ago."

Who are we trying to impress? The only person that matters is God — and He already has all the facts.

4. We call for a reformation in the standards of morality portrayed by the media.

The battle between public decency and media immorality presents a variety of conflicts. For example, do the ratings of motion pictures cause producers to add violence and sex to sell more tickets? And what about a public that wants government out of their lives?

Do they also want to legislate censorship and control?

Public outcry is far more effective than legislation. We will not see the moral standards of the media raised until millions of average citizens vote with their pocket books — when they stop purchasing the products of corporations that sponsor unacceptable programming and refrain from spending money for lewd material.

At the same time, we call for a declaration by media leaders that they raise the standards of morality rather than cater to the tastes of a depraved minority.

God's Word tells us:

> • "Have no fellowship with the unfruitful works of darkness, but rather expose them" (Eph. 5:11).
> • "Do not love the world or the things in the world. If anyone loves the world, the love of the Father is not in him" (1 John 2:15).
> • "Do not let your heart envy sinners, but in the fear of the Lord continue all day long" (Prov. 23:17).

5. We call for a reformation in the example parents set before children.

Mothers and fathers have only one chance to influence their young sons and daughters. The pattern of behavior is set much younger than we realize. For example, 85 percent of our values for life are established by the time we are six years of age. And our personality is formed much earlier.

Every action or reaction makes a permanent imprint. Scripture tell us, "The righteous man walks in his integrity; his children are blessed after him" (Prov. 20:7).

With the writer of the epistle of John, you should say, "I have no greater joy than to hear that my children walk in truth" (3 John 1:4).

6. We call for a reformation in the business practices of God's people.

I am appalled that some people in places of leadership are known to be bad credit risks. Their lack of sound financial judgment affects their ministry. Far too many times trusted leaders have embarked on gigantic projects that have become enormous financial burdens, even to the point of bankruptcy. Why do they operate solely on faith and use other people's money — rarely their own?

One leader, after borrowing millions of dollars to fund his dream, publicly stated, "God has given me the vision. If you do not respond you are out of God's will."

The project collapsed, impacting not only donors, but investors who had lost their capital.

At PTL there were times we were given sound advice by bankers, accountants and attorneys but we often failed to listen. Was the vision all that mattered?

Several years ago, as a denominational official, I was approached by the elders of a church who had discovered that the information on their pastor's resume was false. When difficulties arose during a church building project, they contacted his former church and discovered the man had grossly inflated his previous earnings in order to obtain a larger salary. They also learned he had falsified his educational background.

In my presence the man was brought before the elders. When faced with the facts his face reddened and he feebly attempted to justify the lies.

Misleading people is a serious matter. It is lying. As I tell people across the nation, "A half truth is a whole lie."

7. We call for a reformation in the way the church conducts its affairs.

There are many excuses for operating in secret. "I wanted to safeguard the person's identity," or "I have to protect the rights of the individual."

In the case of church discipline those excuses may be justified, but secrecy is also a mask for incompetence and a shelter for shame.

Once, when I became pastor of a church, I asked to meet with the treasurer to become better acquainted with the accounting procedures. After he had postponed several meetings we finally got together. I had never seen anything like it. In a 25-cent notebook were pages of scribbled numbers only he could decipher. "Don't you think I came up with a pretty good system?" he asked me.

Considering the loose manner in which some ministries and churches are operated, is criticism — both internal and external — justified?

The manner in which a church conducts its business should be open to any member who desires to inquire. I know of no reason, however, that the individual tithes and offerings of members should be made public. That is a private matter between the donor, the church, and the Lord.

Secrets have a way of exposing themselves. I remember walking into a pastor's office after being a Sunday morning guest speaker. He and his wife were personally counting the tithes and offerings on a large table in the center of the room. I later learned they had convinced the congregation that all of the tithes should go to the pastor and the offerings would operate the church.

There was no accounting. No one had the slightest idea of how much was being given. Before long the IRS became involved. Because of the lack of accountability, the pastor was asked to leave and the name of the church was severely damaged in the community.

Scripture tells us that "judgment must begin at the house of God" (1 Pet. 4:17).

8. We call for a reformation in the accountability of non-profit organizations.

Good stewardship demands that educational, charitable, and religious organizations need to commit themselves to the highest standards of accountability.

Recently, I tried to recall just one chief executive I had known who voluntarily disclosed their total income as a matter of public record. I could not think of one. Oh, there were those who listed their salary as $25,000 per year, but they were living a lifestyle that demanded much more than that amount. Something just didn't add up.

Do leaders want the public to know about bonuses, vested annual payments to real estate that will be transferred to their name, and myriad financial plans?

To say that "people wouldn't understand" is wrong. After all, what is the basic source of the funding? It is the people.

External accountability is not enough. Anyone can create a set of books. We need bookkeeping that is based on truth and integrity. We need leadership based on servanthood. May we all listen soberly to the words of the apostle Peter: "Shepherd the flock of God which is among you, serving as overseers, not by compulsion but willingly, not for dishonest gain but eagerly; nor as being lords over those entrusted to you, but being examples to the flock" (1 Pet. 5:2-3).

To present resolutions and change bylaws in order to demand disclosure is not the way to resolve this issue. Let every leader look at his or her own heart. Is their reluctance to disclose because of shame?

I am asking you to join me in this call for a reformation of honesty, integrity, and truth.

On the final page of this book is a declaration with the title "Commitment to Truth." I ask that you prayerfully read the statement. If you can identify with it and will promise before God that your life will be based on truth, please place your signature on the form.

I would also be honored if you would send me a copy of the commitment so that I may personally pray that God will give you the courage to find, to live, and to speak the truth.

Prayer of Affirmation

Our Father, Help me to live in truth. May I walk humbly, with nothing hidden in my life that could bring shame to you, to my family, or myself. Grant that I may walk with you in transparency of heart and conduct. Teach me thy ways, O Lord.

Amen.

Commitment to Truth

With God's help I will commit myself
to live my life in honesty and truth.

- I will acknowledge my faults and ask
    forgiveness.
- I will seek help when I need it.
- I will follow Christ who is the way,
    the truth, and the life.
- I will live a life of open disclosure,
    preventing secrets that will bring
    me shame.

_____

Your signature

_____

Richard W. Dortch
President, Life Challenge

_____

Date

If you so desire, please detach this form and send it to:

Life Challenge
Box 2558
Clearwater, FL 34617

Notes

Chapter 1

[1]James Patterson and Peter Kim, *The Day America Told the Truth* (New York, NY: Prentice-Hall, 1991), p. 7.

[2]Patterson and Kim, *The Day America Told the Truth,* p. 200.

[3]M. Hirsh Goldberg, *The Book of Lies* (New York, NY: Quill/ William Morrow, 1990), p. 6.

[4]Goldberg, *The Book of Lies,* p.15.

[5]Norman Isaacs, *Untended Gates: The Mismanaged Press* (New York, NY: Columbia University Press, 1982), p. 62.

Chapter 2

[1]Sissela Bok, *Lying* (New York, NY: Pantheon Books, 1978), p. 25.

Chapter 4

[1]Frank Minirth and Paul Meier, *The Complete Life Encyclopedia* (Nashville, TN: Thomas Nelson Publishers, 1995), p. 540.

Chapter 5

[1]Leighton Ford, *Transforming Leadership,* (Downers Grove, IL: InterVarsity Press, 1991), p. 151.

[2]"I Made Mistakes," *Christianity Today*, March 18, 1988, p. 46.

[3]Lloy Cory, *Quote Unquote* (Wheaton, IL: Victor Books, 1977), p. 255.

[4]R. David Thomas, *Dave's Way* (New York, NY: G. P. Putnam, 1991), p. 212.

Chapter 7

[1]R. T. Kendall, *God Meant it for Good* (Charlotte, NC: MorningStar Publications, 1988), p. 253.

Chapter 9

[1]Sisella Bok, *Secrets* (New York, NY: Pantheon Books, 1982), p. 70.

Chapter 11

[1]Richard J. Foster, *Prayer* (San Francisco, CA: Harper San Francisco, 1992), p. 142.

[2]"Friendship with Jesus."

Chapter 12

[1]Chris Thurman, *The Lies We Believe* (Nashville, TN: Thomas Nelson Publishers, 1989), p. 163.

Chapter 13

[1]Steve Stecklow, "How New Era's Boss Led Rich and Gullible Into a Web of Deceit," *Wall Street Journal*, May 19, 1995, p. A3.

[2]Stecklow, p. A8.

[3]Larry Burkett, *Business by the Book* (Nashville, TN: Thomas Nelson, Inc., 1990), p. 76.

[4]Susan Terkel, *Ethics* (New York, NY: Lodestar Books, 1992), p. 3.

[5]Mark McCormack, *What They Don't Teach You at Harvard Business School* (New York, NY: Bantam Books, 1984), p. 37.

[6]Glenn Van Ekeren, *Speaker's Sourcebook II* (Englewood Cliff, NJ: Prentice Hall, 1994), p. 193

Chapter 14

[1]Chris Thurman, *The Lies We Believe* (Nashville, TN: Thomas Nelson Publishers, 1989), p. 168.

[2]David Wells, *No Place for Truth* (Grand Rapids, MI: William B. Eerdmans Publishing Co., 1993), p. 282.

[3]Glenn Van Ekeren, *Speaker's Sourcebook II* (Englewood Cliffs, NJ: Prentice-Hall, 1994), p. 194.

Chapter 15

[1]C. Albert Tindley, "Nothing Between."

Chapter 16

[1]George Will, *The Morning After* (New York, NY: Macmillan Publishing, 1987), p. 223.

[2]William J. Bennett, *The Book of Virtues* (New York, NY: Simon & Schuster, 1993), p. 14.

Index

Other books by Richard W. Dortch

Integrity

Fatal Conceit

Losing It All and Finding Yourself

Caring Enough to Help the One You Love

Available from bookstores nationwide
or write

New Leaf Press
P.O. Box 311
Green Forest, AR 72638